MIRRORS

Recent Canadian Verse selected by Jon Pearce

Gage Educational Publishing Limited

Designed by Margot Carter

Photographs by Judy Wilson

Cover design, after *Sunrise* by Margot Carter

ISBN 0-7715-1149-3

COPYRIGHT © GAGE EDUCATIONAL PUBLISHING LIMITED 1975
PRINTED AND BOUND IN CANADA

contents

3 the sound and fury of a metallic sea: poems about city life

4 living on the edges: poems about alienation

5 the progress of barbarism:
poems of satire and social criticism

6 portraits: poems about people

7 kinds of loving: poems about love

8 the poem is for all things: poems about poetry

9 withdrawing from the fire:
poems about old age and death

introduction

All of the poems in this collection have been written by native Canadian poets or by poets who now live in Canada. The majority of the selections have appeared in the last two decades, and nearly all of the poets are actively writing and publishing at the present time. One of the main strengths of this anthology, then, is that the poetry is of our time and relevant to our time.

To sort out and assign places to all the people making poems in Canada is not an easy job, but I would like to suggest four groups of poets who could be called "recent" or "modern" or "contemporary." One group consists of our older, well-established writers, the members of Canada's so-called literary establishment. Another group is made up of those writers who have gained their reputations during the last fifteen years or so. Yet another includes those poets whose work has not been accorded the recognition it deserves; a number of this group have been publishing for some time, while others are just beginning to find their way into print. The fourth group involves those poets writing in French whose work is scarcely known outside their native Quebec. Although we have been fortunate in having a good deal of French-Canadian prose available in English translation, we have not been so lucky with the poetry of Quebec. This book is genuinely Canadian in that it has a substantial representation of our French-Canadian poets, some of whose verse has been translated into English here for the first time.

The anthology, then, is bound together by its subject matter—the poetry written by Canadians during the last twenty years. In addition, the book is internally organized in terms of its themes. I have chosen nine themes or subjects which I think are especially important to human experience: youth, nature, city life, alienation, satire, people, love, poetry, and old age and death. Within each section, the poems are strategically organized so as to complement each other, while the sections themselves are ordered to create a logical and coherent whole

Any anthology involves to a greater or lesser extent the personal preferences of its editor, and *Mirrors* is no exception: the poems here are poems that I like. But at the same time, they are poems that I think the reader will like. What I have not done—or at least what I have tried to avoid—is to include any of the old war-horses that are regularly and monotonously anthologized.

The poems in this book are accessible but not simple; they lend themselves to close textual analysis in a classroom or library but can simply be read and enjoyed on a bus or in a park. This anthology, I hope, charts out the various distinctive contours of the contemporary Canadian landscape. Perhaps this is the first purpose of *Mirrors:* to offer to the student, teacher, and general reader a collection of poems that testifies to the adventure and excitement of the verse being written by Canadians who are writing now.

J.P.
Upper Canada College
July, 1974

1
down swift years:
poems about growing up

The poems in this section deal with youth, growing up, and the passing of time. In each of these poems it is possible to see two distinct points of view: that of the child inside the poem and that of the poet outside the poem. The attitude of children is an unself-conscious one; heedlessly they rush "laughing / down / swift / years," R. G. Everson tells us. The child is unaware that youth is ever departing, that beauty is a fragile and perishable commodity, that innocence is inescapably being supplanted by experience. In a sense, the life of the child is lived from the inside out. Children live life more as subjects than as objects; they are interested only in the self-centered pursuit of the immediate, sensuous experience of their day-to-day lives.

The perspective of the poet who has written the poem is markedly different, however. From the vantage point of maturity, the poet sees the child from the outside in, not as a subject but as an object. The perception of the poet in some cases is that the process of growing up is accompanied by self-discovery and knowledge. In Bill Howell's poem, for example, the afternoon of the maturation process comes only when each of the young boys finds a "different name" for himself. And the speaker in "Counter-Signs" concludes that "At last I know where I am" — although he ironically adds that "I am nowhere at all." Finally, James Reaney's poem moves to a harsh and bitter conclusion: his childhood was not one of "pleasant skies," as he once believed, but, as he now recognizes, was a world filled with "blood, pus, horror, death, stepmothers, and lies." Each of the poems in this section, then, juxtaposes the worlds of youth and age and, from the detached point of view of the poet, comments on the meaning of the journey from one world to the other.

The Philosophers

```
                    ladders
          park        then
          play
        high                slide
        climb
        slowly                    laughing
      they
      while                          down
    nervously
  wave                                swift
Children                                years
```

R. G. Everson

Song for Naomi

Who is that in the tall grasses singing
By herself, near the water?
I can not see her
But can it be her
Than whom the grasses so tall
Are taller,
My daughter,
My lovely daughter?

Who is that in the tall grasses running
Beside her, near the water?
She can not see there
Time that pursued her
In the deep grasses so fast
And faster
And caught her,
My foolish daughter.

What is the wind in the fair grass saying
Like a verse, near the water?
Saviors that over
All things have power
Make Time himself grow kind
And kinder
That sought her,
My little daughter.

Who is that at the close of the summer
Near the deep lake? Who wrought her
Comely and slender?
Time but attends and befriends her
Than whom the grasses though tall
Are not taller,
My daughter,
My gentle daughter.

Irving Layton

High Heels

Little girl from next door
in your mother's high heels
oceans too big for you,
yet managing somehow
to edge down the sidewalk.

Too soon you'll have
a pair all your own
to show off those legs,
leaving childhood behind
with the kindling shape of them.

Right now I want
those small running feet
with the silk hair above,
the face full of wonder.

You'll be old soon enough,
your beauty a trouble
to all those who see you,
your manner self-conscious,
so terribly proud,

little girl going by
with the click-clack-clatter
of your mother's heels
walking hard on my heart.

Raymond Souster

Adolescence

In love they wore themselves in a green embrace.
A silken rain fell through the spring upon them.
In the park she fed the swans and he
whittled nervously with his strange hands.
And white was mixed with all their colours
as if they drew it from the flowering trees.

At night his two-finger whistle brought her down
the waterfall stairs to his shy smile
which, like an eddy, turned her round and round
lazily and slowly so her will
was nowhere — as in dreams things are and aren't.

Strolling along avenues in the dark
street lamps sang like sopranos in their heads
with a violence they never understood
and all their movements when they were together
had no conclusion.

Only leaning into the question had they motion;
after they parted were savage and swift as gulls.
Asking and asking the hostile emptiness
they were as sharp as partly sculptured stone
and all who watched, forgetting, were amazed
to see them form and fade before their eyes.

P. K. Page

Boys and Dogs

Boys bark, too. Twice I was the Black Fox,
and Charlie Richardson was the only guy allowed
to be it three times because he broke his arm,

and Hatfield, and Brother Bob, and Syd Dumaresq,
and Cammy Robinson, and Wilsie and Steve and
Denny Perlin and everyone
was Red or Blue or White or Yellow or Green
or Purple and even Silver or Gold Fox.

It was understood that we each took our own turn.

Arriving on blue-and-white CCM bikes
in any of three speeds with no licenses,
leaving Miss Ferguson's fraction problems behind
the whole unreasonable wonder of the woods. . . .

Other times we made the dogs play dead, dug holes
in the clearing in the part of the woods

behind Billy McKinnon's house, just when his mother
always seemed to have some new brown bread, and played

marbles. We spent whole mornings shooting glass balls
in the sunlight, and the game ended only

when there were too many rules, only
when it became necessary to name it.

Chopping and peeling up and down alders and our
Saturday mornings with soon-to-be-lost jack-knives,

chomping through ten o'clock apples
in not-so-secret spruce forts. . . .

Maybe it was because there were no girls allowed.

Maybe it was the girls that were our ultimate
discovery, the one that made the question of the game
hardly worth playing, afterwards.

Maybe we only made so many great discoveries
because there were greater ones to be made.

Maybe we did grow up in those Saturday suns,
and afternoons only came when each of us
found a different name for himself.

Bill Howell

Prairie Grade School

Even now, we entered quietly, afraid
to interrupt and wondering about the
unlocked door. Later we would speak of
the broken water cooler, covered with dust
and the tracks of mice, of the word
scratched with a nail on the blackboard, of
the smell of damp earth and rot. We had
almost expected this. Still, no one
would mention how we were surprised not so much
by the dead meadowlark in the broken window
as by its silence . . .

In this room, it is easy to remember
the broken legs, the new swear words, the
election of Louis St. Laurent. Here we sat
in rows, memorizing rules that were intended
to last for life; our teachers, young ladies
from Neepawa or bigger towns a great distance away,
always to the south. I was here on the day
things first changed, the day I hid from friends
who learned to play without me, discovering
I controlled nothing and growing afraid
for the first time of ordinary trees . . .

From the distance of less than a mile,
nothing seems changed. The building,
standing at a crossroads (one road
goes nowhere, another the only road
to the last farmer before the bush begins),
still colonizes the half acre of land
seven immigrant fathers and a municipal clerk
stole from the prairie. It remains,
useful only as landmark. And landmark
·to none but the homecoming sons of farmers.

Dale Zieroth

Autobiographical

Out of the ghetto streets where a Jewboy
Dreamed pavement into pleasant Bible-land,
Out of the Yiddish slums where childhood met
The friendly beard, the loutish Sabbath-goy,
Or followed, proud, the Torah-escorting band,
Out of the jargoning city I regret,
Rise memories, like sparrows rising from
The gutter-scattered oats,
Like sadness sweet of synagogal hum,
Like Hebrew violins
Sobbing delight upon their Eastern notes.

Again they ring their little bells, those doors
Deemed by the tender-year'd, magnificent.
Old Ashkenazi's cellar, sharp with spice;
The widows' double-parlored candy-stores
And nuggets sweet bought for one sweaty cent;
The warm fresh-smelling bakery, its pies,
Its cakes, its navel'd bellies of black bread;
The lintels candy-poled
Of barber-shop, bright-bottled, green, blue, red;
And fruit-stall piled, exotic,
And the big synagogue door, with letters of gold.

Again my kindergarten home is full —
Saturday night — with kin and compatriot:
My brothers playing Russian card-games; my
Mirroring sisters looking beautiful,
Humming the evening's imminent fox-trot;
My uncle Mayer, of blessed memory,
Still murmuring *maariv*, counting holy words;
And the two strangers, come
Fiery from Volhynia's murderous hordes —
The cards and humming stop.
And I too swear revenge for that pogrom.

9

Occasions dear: the four-legged *aleph* named
And angel pennies dropping on my book;
The rabbi patting a coming scholar-head;
My mother, blessing candles, Sabbath-flamed,
Queenly in her Warsovian perruque;

My father pickabacking me to bed
To tell tall tales about the Baal Shem Tov —
Letting me curl his beard.
Oh memory of unsurpassing love,
Love leading a brave child
Through childhood's ogred corridors, unfear'd!

The week in the country at my brother's — (May
He own fat cattle in the fields of heaven!)
Its picking of strawberries from grassy ditch,
Its odour of dogrose and of yellowing hay —
Dusty, adventurous, sunny days, all seven! —
Still follow me, still warm me, still are rich
With the cow-tinkling peace of pastureland.
The meadow'd memory
Is sodded with its clover, and is spanned
By that same pillow'd sky
A boy on his back one day watched enviously.

And paved again the street: the shouting boys,
Oblivious of mothers on the stoops,
Playing the robust robbers and police,
The corncob battle — all high-spirited noise
Competitive among the lot-drawn groups.
Another day, of shaken apple trees
In the rich suburbs, and a furious dog,
And guilty boys in flight;
Hazelnut games, and games in the synagogue —
The burrs, the Haman rattle,
The Torah dance on Simchas Torah night.

Immortal days of the picture calendar
Dear to me always with the virgin joy
Of the first flowering of senses five,
Discovering birds, or textures, or a star,
Or tastes sweet, sour, acid, those that cloy;
And perfumes. Never was I more alive.
All days thereafter are a dying off,
A wandering away
From home and the familiar. The years doff
Their innocence.
No other day is ever like that day.

I am no old man fatuously intent
On memories, but in memory I seek
The strength and vividness of nonage days,
Not tranquil recollection of event.
It is a fabled city that I seek;
It stands in Space's vapours and Time's haze;
Thence comes my sadness in remembered joy
Constrictive of the throat;
Thence do I hear, as heard by a Jewboy,
The Hebrew violins,
Delighting in the sobbed Oriental note.

A. M. Klein

Chronology

I was born senile and gigantic
my wrinkles charting
in pink the heights and ruts, events
of all possible experience.

At 6 I was sly as a weasel,
adroit at smiling and hiding,
slippery-fingered, greasy with guile.

At 12, instructed
by the comicbooks already
latent in my head, I was bored with horror.

At 16 I was pragmatic,
armoured with wry lipstick;
I was invulnerable,
I wore my hair like a helmet.

But by 20 I had begun
to shed knowledge like petals
or scales; and today I discovered
that I have been living backwards.

Time wears me down like water.
The engraved lines of my features
are being slowly expunged.

I will have to pretend:
the snail knows
thin skin is no protection;

though I can't go on
indefinitely. At 50 they will peel
my face away like a nylon stocking

uncovering such incredible blank
innocence, that even mirrors
accustomed to grotesques
will be astounded.

I will be unshelled, I will be
of no use to that city
and like a horse with a broken back
I will have to be taken out and shot.

Margaret Atwood

Counter-Signs

By moving West
I learned how to go East.
By standing on my head
I found out the importance of feet.
Through stumbling
I discovered dancing,
Through slaughter,
Kindness.
Wanting to go somewhere
I started in the other direction.
At last I know where I am.
I am nowhere at all.

F. R. Scott

Any Man's History

Any man's history, or any girl's
is a sequence of such moments . . .
waiting in a station,
scanning the newspaper or poetry magazine,

hearing of the death
of someone
you hardly knew,
and feeling,
as you climb the stairs,
older . . .

Any man's life story, or any girl's
is a series of those moments
after the hands touch,
after the doors are closed
and the chairs
turned upside down,
four on each similar table . . .

is a
goodnight, and walking home
by cold, white light.

Our footsteps echo,
echo
in the future,
and with each living breath
we practise death.

Ian Young

The Child I Was

All that remains of childhood's fire
Is one burnt stone
And a thing that sometimes watches me
                        through nocturnal eyes,
A little ghost
In the pleading landscape,
A child over there, the child I was, maybe . . .

Marie-Claire Blais

Translated from the French by John Glassco

The School Globe

Sometimes when I hold
Our faded old globe
That we used at school
To see where oceans were
And the five continents,
The lines of latitude and longitude,
The North Pole, the Equator and the South Pole —
Sometimes when I hold this
Wrecked blue cardboard pumpkin
I think: here in my hands
Rest the fair fields and lands
Of my childhood
Where still lie or still wander
Old games, tops and pets;
A house where I was little
And afraid to swear
Because God might hear and
Send a bear
To eat me up;

Rooms where I was as old
As I was high;
Where I loved the pink clenches,
The white, red and pink fists
Of roses; where I watched the rain
That Heaven's clouds threw down
In puddles and rutfuls
And irregular mirrors
Of soft brown glass upon the ground.
This school globe is a parcel of my past,
A basket of pluperfect things.
And here I stand with it
Sometime in the summertime
All alone in an empty schoolroom
Where about me hang
Old maps, an abacus, pictures,
Blackboards, empty desks.
If I raise my hand
No tall teacher will demand
What I want.
But if someone in authority
Were here, I'd say
Give me this old world back
Whose husk I clasp
And I'll give you in exchange
The great sad real one
That's filled
Not with a child's remembered and pleasant skies,
But with blood, pus, horror, death, step-mothers, and lies.

James Reaney

2

a beauty of dissonance:
poems about nature

Historically, the world of nature has exercised a powerful influence on the creative energies of the Canadian writer. This is no less true today than it was a century ago, when the pioneer was still struggling to gain a foothold in a new and difficult environment. Then, the natural world was perhaps the single most important presence that stimulated the imaginations of our writers. But even now, in our urban-centered society and in the face of a diminishing wilderness, the Canadian poet frequently turns to the world of nature for the subject matter of his verse.

The manner of his response is not single or simple. The natural world elicits a wide range and variety of responses, as the poems in this section demonstrate. At one extreme, the modern, urban poet may regard the landscape as hostile; accordingly, Ian Young looks upon it as something to be feared and avoided. At the other extreme, a poet may be impressed by the elemental grandeur and beauty of nature, and find in it a source of esthetic pleasure, peace, and comfort: Earle Birney says as much in "Daybreak on Lake Opal." Or the writer's response may be ambivalent. For Genevieve Bartole and A. J. M. Smith, the world of nature is a blend of the positive and negative: it is both creative and destructive, congenial and alien. In other cases, when the world outside is viewed with objectivity and detachment, the poet suggests that the ongoing process of nature has an independence and integrity of its own; F. R. Scott, for example, concludes that it belongs wholly to itself and obeys its own laws. These various attitudes and responses—and more—are all present and working in the poems that follow.

Spring

The day cries fete
A bird swoops low
And all the sky
Beats in its wing

The Spring eddies
From fresh veins
Making known
Their secret joys

While April's
Tender eye-lashes
Tremble one last
Glitter of frost

Alma de Chantal

Translated from the French by Fred Cogswell

Arctic Spring

Arctic spring:
First flash of gulls against frozen sea,
Shrieks in soundless air.

Northern landscape:
Vistas of rose and mauve light
Shimmering on sea ice.

David Keenleyside

Breakup

Ice Lens
of the river

breaking open,
how coldly it regards me!

Frazil over mushweed
where the pickerel lurk.
All winter they have evaded
the rod of the ice fisherman
and light spilled
        through a hole
in their sleep.

Now
the breakup threatens
to let them through
        to the surface.
A far sea roars.

Can the wild goose hear it
        flying over the river?
See it?
And the cat know it
sniffing bird tracks
        in the last snow?

O God, I am not like a cat—
to take into the night
light borrowed from the day.
What I see are shadows in motion,
and of such deep substance,
        white world, bleeding
shadows, dark

As the darkness of water.
Moving nearer its edge I see
a deer of such indescribable beauty
it must surely travel the river forever
embalmed in an ice floe.
Its antlers make its own gray
   headstone.

Ice-stitched carcass:
—did only a raven, perhaps
back in the forest
   witness the lost footing
the hurtle over the bank?
Only the sun see how life runs
slowly out of the mouth
   in freezing?

Till the moon rose
and in your glassy eyeball
   reflected again
the gray-green tents of treetops
the moving brunt panorama
   of bank and boulder.

Now it is over.
You have come so far. And though
   there is mercy tonight
in an east wind
the river's mouth has little taste
   for you yet
stuffed as it is with ice
   and brown weed water.

Genevieve Bartole

Mackenzie River

This river belongs
　　wholly to itself
　　　　obeying its own laws

Its wide brown eye
　　softens what it reflects
　　　　from sky and shore

The top water　　calm
　　moves purposefully
　　　　to a cold sea

Underneath　　its stone bed
　　shows sunken rock
　　　　in swirl and surface wave

Suspended
　　in its liquid force
　　　　is the soil of deltas

The servient valleys
　　reach up to lake and spring
　　　　in clefts of far hills

And shed
　　arteries of streams
　　　　that stain the central flood

In spring thaw and spate
　　its wide levels
　　　　rise slowly　　fall

Like tides
   that start upstream
      and die at sea

A river so Canadian
   it turns its back
      on America

The Arctic shore
   receives the vast flow
      a maze of ponds and dikes

In land so bleak and bare
   a single plume of smoke
      is a scroll of history.

F. R. Scott

The River

The river's long unfinished sentence
on the lips of the gulf
like a wound in this country's hip
and the islands dreaming of drifts and adventures
cannot bear to stay
all bent back on the words to come

Between the steep banks of its solitude
the river seeks only a dream
forever unmindful of memory
drowning it over and over
in the current of fecund waters
like molten sunlight

At the beginning of a song both new and long restrained
the river
with its thousand voices like one voice
and its mists like sails spread
in the full noon of its advent.

Marcel Bélanger

Translated from the French by H. Porter Abbott

Daybreak on Lake Opal: High Rockies

as
the
fire
from
opals
a trem
-ulous
dawn be-
gins its
ceremony of
s l o w touch
without palms
its breath with-
out breathing along
the whorled turrets
moving shimmering fall
-ing over the scarred for
-ever-by-the-wind-besieged
ramparts the icecracked tree-
breached walls   the light of
the untouchable Sun sliding from
skyblue into the chill broken flesh
of our lifedrop   warming freeing the
silence of jays and firtops   sending a
heather of wind over unfolding asters and
eaglets   ruffling the moated lake to a green
soul and rolling once more the upraised sacrifice
of our world into the sword of Its   P R E S E N C E

Earle Birney

August, the Moon of Ripe Berries

Late August, and the trail mud
getting harder, the better going
pounded flat by horses and deer
Half asleep in the steep ascent
the thud of hooves rouses me
A brown bear, full of loganberries
rattles the steaming thickets in his course

Duchesnay Lake trail
free of the water now
Pack horse nipping at my wheezing pony

They stiffen, ears up
as a rutting moose charges
knee high through the blue shallows
behind us, a horny juvenile
kicking up rainbows
cooling in Duchesnay water

Rank mooshwa in their nostrils
spooks the horses, I speak softly
dance through a tangle of deadfalls
push in my spurs
The gelding rolls his eye backward
and shows his sage old teeth

He remembers the elbow
in his ribs yesterday
when he stepped on my foot
He still has much to teach me
and I have a lump for each lesson

High water has choked the trail with snags
My last chore in the summer ending
bucking the snags by Duchesnay water

The chainsaw breathes a blue smoke
cool air fills with the roar of the motor
horses sleep on their feet
The bear comes to see them
they are not impressed
runs off when the saw stops, coughing

At the end of the meadow
the lake subsides in a wind
Spruce needles fall from the boughs
where my mare rubs her cheek
on the rough, sticky bark
showering the upturned petals
of the orange paintbrush

The bear returns from his solitary harvest
prowling across my tracks
smelling the ripeness
of big spruce, toppled and broken
three feet thick, promise of beetles
of spruce budworms, like fat white plums

In the quiet now
is the continuous pattering
of ripe fruit falling
on the thick duff
the forest floor

Sid Marty

Banff

The skiers dwindle up out of the valley.
The deft wind skims the snow
and with a sudden shift of temper
snarls and snaps at the puffy twigs
    spilling their whiteness on the blue-white drifts
        in patterns pencil-blue.
The long pines lean into the sky. Chalk-blue
the blank sky stares. Anthracite hill
    is blazing white on Tunnel's further flank
and Cascade blazing keen into the sun,
and white spume curls, clenches the green-blue Bow,
    the milk-green, solid-sliding, weltered Bow . . .
Savage hauteur, accepting cyclic Time
as but the lidding of a frozen Eye. . . .

Margaret Avison

Canadian January Night

Ice storm: the hill
a pyramid of black crystal
down which the cars
slide like phosphorescent beetles
while I, walking backwards in obedience
to the wind, am possessed
of the fearful knowledge
my compatriots share
but almost never utter:
this is a country
where a man can die
                    simply from being
caught outside.

Alden Nowlan

Fear of the Landscape

On a hot morning
walking through rough thicket,
bushes and rocks
close to the bluffs
I was uneasy and clung to things.
The sound of a cricket
or the calls of birds were shrill
lesions in the quiet air
around me, sweltering and still.
The leaves hung from the trees
dangling on thin stems.

I am walking quickly and the land
stops. The ground
drops to a beach of stones
where a silent boat leans at the shore
into a sandy mound,
its stiff poled oars
outstretched.
The lake gulls circling it
cry out in the heat.
The sound of dry breath clings to me.
I hear the sun's core burn.
Have I been too long in cities
that I have such fear
of the landscape?

Ian Young

Landscape Estranged

The storm raged about
and the snow blew into our breast
right in the breast
crowned with pain-sharp ice
crowned with thorns
love words driven into the brow

great storm before our eyes in a world estranged
every night tore a cry from us
and we grew up in agony
slowly we were aging
and the landscape aged with us—against us

the landscape was no longer the same
the landscape was sombre
the landscape no longer fitted us like a glove
no longer had the colors of our youth
the landscape the beautiful landscape was no longer beautiful
there were no more streams
no more ferns no water
there was nothing left

the landscape had to be remade.

Roland Giguère

Translated from the French by F. R. Scott

I No Longer Believe . . .

I no longer believe in what I don't know about cities, but
there's still something in open country and clear deep water
that draws me. Because I fear to know: knowledge of something attractive only in its enigma is terrible. That sweet small
darkness is going away as I return and return and cannot
but return. I turn to this tangled landscape as a man turns to
a woman and dream that because I haven't been here before,
neither has any other man.

J. Michael Yates

The Lonely Land

Cedar and jagged fir
uplift sharp barbs
against the gray
and cloud-piled sky;
and in the bay
blown spume and windrift
and thin, bitter spray
snap
at the whirling sky;
and the pine trees
lean one way.

A wild duck calls
to her mate,
and the ragged
and passionate tones
stagger and fall,
and recover,
and stagger and fall,
on these stones—
are lost
in the lapping of water
on smooth, flat stones.

This is a beauty
of dissonance,
this resonance
of stony strand,
this smoky cry
curled over a black pine
like a broken
and wind-battered branch
when the wind
bends the tops of the pines
and curdles the sky
from the north.
This is the beauty
of strength
broken by strength
and still strong.

A. J. M. Smith

3

the sound and fury of a metallic sea:

poems about city life

The poems about urban life in this section reveal a deep-seated paradox: we choose to live in our cities, yet at the same time we hate them. Almost without exception, the epithets and images that inform and dominate these poems speak of futility, defeat, and death — emotional and spiritual, if not physical. Indeed, as David Helwig tells us, we often name our cities "as a way of naming death."

Granted, the city is not always imaged as a kind of Dantean underworld. Jean-Guy Pilon compares the city to a beautiful woman, and George Johnston speaks of the city covered by a "great roof of pity." Still, it is the dark side of city life that persists and persuades and constitutes the imaginative centre of the poems that follow. While at one time, long past, perhaps during some dimly remembered or imagined Golden Age, we were all beautiful and believing, now, as Jean-Paul Filion insists, we have become victims of "the sound and fury of a metallic sea," corroded by "the acid heart of an inflamed city."

Cities

We name them often as a way of naming death,
the hard death of concrete, all the deaths that can be died
alone as men turn their heads, passing, and puzzle themselves
with what to think or say as the light of splendour
falls away from the flesh and death names itself on the lips
of the falling man. We name them for the crowd
of men that die there each day, as the pale yellow
haze hangs in the air like bad music and the cars
tear off the fingers of silence and the signs flash and quiver
like the involuntary shudders of a seizure,
the lights declare their colors like a man declaring his hatred.
We name them dead, dying, because we cannot think
of what we know, because there are so many souls we'll
    never have,
bodies we'll never love, and the cost of money gets higher
    every day.

And the cities darken, the concrete hardens and narrows, a
    man walking
sees nothing but walls, and the child is soothed
by engines throbbing and suckled on the sour reek of the air
until his throat burns and reddens as he grows to find
that his feet are anchored in cement, that he can only
stand still and watch the gray walls hunt him down
until he would be glad of a coffin for space, of death for
    silence.

The cities darken. We name them death and go from
    drive-in to drive-in
locked in our cars. And down at the centre
the dark is darkest, the air has been stolen
and sold, and as we bend under the weight of buildings
and eat our money, we open our sore red eyes
and see at our feet in darkness a movement, a presence that
    is sudden
and mysterious, a bug presence, bug self, the dwarf soul

that we have harboured and ignored, and in a small hoarse
    voice
the bug self says "You, useless citizen, who voted
for ecstasy and then wondered what it meant,
citizen of longing, subtle policeman, you alderman of new
    clothes,
I register my approval of all you never did,
the killer you hesitated to worship, the regret at the edge
of action. Citizen of regret, passenger, the movies are free
    and sexy,
but once you ignored the screen and took the hand
of the sad giant beside you who wept with a soft sound
like the rustling of bedclothes. Once, friend, on the bus
in the early morning you looked in a window and saw
a man standing beside a table, once in a junkyard, the light
caught a discarded chrome bumper and made you blink.
Citizen of forever, there is a darkness between your toes
    where the amoeba
may begin once more his ascent into the murderous cities.
Citizen of regret, the city is darkness on the face
of the deep and God has not yet commanded it to be."

David Helwig

The City Planners

Cruising these residential Sunday
streets in dry August sunlight:
what offends us is
the sanities:
the houses in pedantic rows, the planted
sanitary trees, assert
levelness of surface like a rebuke
to the dent in our car door.
No shouting here, or
shatter of glass; nothing more abrupt
than the rational whine of a power mower
cutting a straight swath in the discouraged grass.

But though the driveways neatly
sidestep hysteria
by being even, the roofs all display
the same slant of avoidance to the hot sky,
certain things;
the smell of spilled oil a faint
sickness lingering in the garages,
a splash of paint on brick surprising as a bruise,
a plastic hose poised in a vicious
coil; even the too-fixed stare of the wide windows

give momentary access to
the landscape behind or under
the future cracks in the plaster

when the houses, capsized, will slide
obliquely into the clay seas, gradual as glaciers
that right now nobody notices.

That is where the City Planners
with the insane faces of political conspirators

are scattered over unsurveyed
territories, concealed from each other,
each in his own private blizzard;
guessing directions, they sketch
transitory lines rigid as wooden borders
on a wall in the white vanishing air

tracing the panic of suburb
order in a bland madness of snows.

Margaret Atwood

City Hall Street

for Irving Layton

In this sweet courtyard of dirt and smells and rot
children play, old men rock in their chairs, and women
hang out the ragged washings of the week. This goes on

winter, summer, fall and spring, year after year,
children playing, old men rocking, women washing,
only it is other children who play, other old men who sit in
        their chairs, other women hanging out clothes.

O this courtyard never changes,
it's still the same dirt, same rot, same smell,
same squirming, crawling tenement, tin-roofed sweat-box on
        the lower slopes of Hell,

open sore on the face of God.

Raymond Souster

Queen Street Trolley

We form jagged rows of bodies and stand now
like a defeated army, with umbrellas, newspapers
and feet as weapons. No one is talking: the trolley
makes all the noise. We have read
and re-read all the ads. We know the shops
by heart, landmarks to count off time: Rubinoff's,
Shumsky's Jewellers, the Public Exchange Mart or
Eaton's with the display window that changes
twice a week and is never twice the same.

There are nearly fifty people here, all
uncomfortable, none familiar or recognized.
The driver continues to insist there is plenty
of room somewhere at the back. Outside the cars
glide by like brilliantly colored birds while we
move from stop to stop like something wounded.

I am an unknown Lenin nearing Moscow, full
of secret plans for change that are half-forgotten
the moment I am out and walking home.

In the house we are surrounded by nothing more
offensive than tv guides and want ads. We have washed
our hands and prepared for the supper that is
a slow ritual of withdrawal. Here it becomes
safe to dream of quitting work two hours early,
walking out, shouting slogans as we leave. Soon
the laughter begins to come more quickly: the things
that move are moved by us. Control returns.

Yet the heaviness remains. We cannot forget
the timeless clock-watching work, bordered morning
and night by the push and smell of bodies. Already
the morning is in sight. We are not yet asleep
when the journey begins again, full of the

stony senselessness that changes nothing, choked with
a thousand small and nasty turns. Each day
is the same and brings us one day closer to the
angry ideology of random targets and stones.

Dale Zieroth

Poem for My Native City

By day, a black inverted drop, a faintly nodding light by night,
I look from unknown angles
at the panorama of our association;
at the shining hummocks of your mercenary engineers,
at the ice-jams of your fibrillar growth,
where the sky blinks steeply down into the north
or pales away in infinite progression across the border
    mountains pushing up like teeth under hard blue gums.
What an effort it is to think about your history
or to teach you the alphabet of a consciousness!
As it is
I and all of us alive
are relics of your past drifting in the currents
of the glass-caverned rivers of your shopping streets.
Where do the river pilots meet so that I may start my
    campaign?
What has happened to the rotting cache, the pulpy mixture
    of your blueprints?
And where do you keep the ice fences? (so that I may smash
    them as a first decisive step).
Each time I've left you I've returned wiser, I think, and more
    detached.
You no longer blockade my mind
as a rough-cut amethyst dipped in coal dust and naphthaline.
The desolation of your outskirts can never close, as it did, its
    ring about the iris of my eye.
The signs of your freight yards no longer lie beneath my
    fractiousness like the candelabra of a new faith.
And I'm cured of the blight of the robot activities of the river

(indifferent perhaps to human pain)
of the ships that pass with chemical bruises
slowly mouthing out an inarticulate black,
consigned to crawl in line as the tumbrils of their own
    extermination.
As a poet, I tell you
that the terminals of your dealings can never substitute for
    the spokes of a star,
that the countless love affairs now taking place in your parlors
are nothing but the meanest genre,
that the petty crimes which pass me daily like the lines of
    random bullets
are careful threads in a tapestry of plastic obliteration.

Eldon Grier

The Ebb Begins From Dream

The stars like stranded starfish pale and die
and tinted sands of dawning dry
The ebb begins from dream   leaving a border
of milk and morning paper on the porches

From crusted reefs of homes   from unkempt shores
the workers slip reluctant   half-asleep
lapse back into the city's deep
The waves of factory hands and heads   of salesman
eyes and waiting waitress faces
slide soughing out from night's brief crannies
suck back along the strand of streets   rattling
pebbled smalltalk.

O then the curves and curls
of girl stenographers   the loops and purls
of children foaming in the ooze
that by the ceaseless moon of living moves
through heaving flats of habit down the day

And late   from tortuous coves   remoter bays
there sets the sinuous undertow
of brokers   and the rolling politicians flow
to welter in the one pelagic motion
Housewives   beached like crabs in staling pools
crisscross   are swashed in search of food
down to the midtown breakers' booming

At last with turning earth   relentless moon
slow but flooding comes the swell once more
with gurge and laughter's plash and murmur
back to the fraying rocks   far-freighted now
with briny flotsam of each morning vow
a wrack of deeds that dulls with neaping
dead thoughts that float again to sea
salt evening weeds that lie
and rot between the cracks of life
and hopes that waterlogged will never link
with land   but will be borne until they sink

Now tide is full and sighing creeps
into the clean sought coigns of sleep
And yet in sleep begins to stir
to mutter in the dark its yearning
and to the round possessive mother turning
dreams of vaster wellings   makes the last cliff totter
cradles all the globe in swaying water

The ebb begins from dream . . . .

Earle Birney

The Work Shift

I gather my crooked work boots
that Christ should have worn
along the road to Golgotha
and the boots have a certain personality,
they're starved from a lack of polish and
broken through from labor, eaten by the very
life's dust, just like some people I know.
I place my warped feet inside the crooked boots.

Every afternoon (except Sat. and Sun.)
the round face of the "Silver Bell" alarm clock
laughs out a prolonged shrill dagger
that mutilates the egg shell world of my dream.
O how I love to sleep, I'm obsessed by sleep,
because I'm tired like those boots.
About 2:30 p.m. I'm out on the street, dragging
my clod-hoppers along the pavement and
I'm aware of the sparrows digging me over
with their J. Edgaring eyes:
at the corner of Avenue Road and Davenport,
the cops are loitering by the bank
like scarabs around a dung heap.

3:00 p.m. I'm at work unloading a C.P. Express trailer
and a wired box prison of miniature ground hogs—
guinea pigs marked up for the cancer factory—
moves along the belt:
so I think the only difference
between me and that family
is that I take a longer road to hell.

Joe Rosenblatt

On Saint-Urbain Street

My room's bigger than a coffin
but not so well made.
The couple on my left drink, and
at two a.m. the old man shouts
of going back to Russia.
About five he or his wrung-out wife
puke up their passage money.

The janitor (pay, five a week
plus a one-bed apartment
with furnace in kitchen) has
one laughing babe at home
and two girls, for lack of room,
in the orphanage.
On holidays they appear
with their soul-smashed faces.

Upstairs the Negro girl
answers the phone, sings my name
in a voice like a bad angel's.
Her boy-friends change
every week-end, like the movies.
But my room's cheap, tho
when the wind shifts north
I wear my overcoat
to type this bitter little poem.

Milton Acorn

La Gare Centrale, Montreal

It is humming half-dark in the station of the wayfarers;
it is strangely dark and it is a late journey
I am taking from the station of the neon stars,
flicking an ancient Nazarene affair in our faces

the slim dark little Frenchwomen come clacking
at heels and tongues across the Concourse—
how is it they stay so mysteriously and unmistakably
feminine while the rest of the continent
de-sexes itself, wears smart gray, essence of neuter?

the smelly simple man beside me, aged forty,
is reading the comics, talking with Superman;
behind me on the telephone a woman, between trains,
is establishing a world record for "d'accord—d'accord—
    d'accord"

the newstand is an anodyne for this reality;
and what shall the piped music do for our separations
as we attend our destinies in the station,
this place of torn flesh and the insufficient kiss?
for EVERYTHING is told in our farewells, the woman
fussing over her impatient grown son and he,
forbearing his ambivalence; the boy hopefully
looking into the eyes of the disapproving father,
turning away then without the necessary sign;
this wife, giving anxiously, and this husband,
receiving in boredom, looking at his escape route
over her shoulders.

two uniformly bizarre and dyed young lovers
like figures on a Swiss Clock circle around
and around the station, holding onto each other
with rigid arms; have they come in out of the cold
to talk and make a big decision or are they looking
for Dan, Dan, the Magic-Man to make it for them?

a fat old woman with swollen feet, carrying a felt bag
and trailing a little complementary shrunken man
moves down to the ticket taker; I think they spoke
before he turned to go but two negatives
do not make a sound, even at the ending.

and now a crazy sailor has broken a bottle
of whisky at the feet of the ticket taker;
his companions are cursing his carelessness
and the onlookers are laughing with Christmas echoes
all through the station of the neon stars.

the sweet smell of twenty-six ounces
of good Scotch whisky arises around us all

we are to be drugged then for this departure
and I lean back on the bench with my heart
like a bent bough and wonder
what we told the others in our farewells here
not so many years ago when sometimes we travelled
whole nights for one hour of mending;
did someone then watching us here perceive
the Sophoclean shadows between us,
the yin and yang of our inherited curse?

the faces crowd past me, outlining their old stories;
the pace quickens — someone is running
with a heavy suitcase
into the netherlands between leaving
and arriving

down the steps to the trains below
they descend like condemned to the underworld

46

they were all once beautiful and believing

and still the green lights of the neon stars
illuminate

our longing

Joan Finnigan

Paris

Like others I plunge my roots
Into the acid heart of an inflamed city
Like every one else I mingle my blood larded
        with foreign soil
In the scarlet broth of a mad capital
Paris!

Paris-volcano
Paris like a hell
A blazing ball of virulent folly
Paris brandishing its sabres under the noses of stars
Wizard-city of heavenly sounds
City of copper avenues plumed with star-fountains
City of pylons on the backs of foreigners
Paris like the sound and fury of a metallic sea
Paris-paris where your accomplice man sets sail
        for the port of the unknown

I swim with short breast-strokes
Ignored, invisible, without a flaw
With the crowd's jazz posted in my mouth
I swim, parading the famine of my eyes
On the salt-peter of walls
In the salt of streets
I swim calmly
In all the power of my granite hope.

Jean-Paul Filion

Translated from the French by Fred Cogswell

O Montreal

Montreal
The only city in the world where the sun sets in the North!
City entirely surrounded by sewers,
     one of which provides the drinking water
Ruled by its ten per cent of English . . .
Where money talks — a refined language
And French bombs explode . . .

Greatest frozen inland port
Second largest English-speaking French city in the world
Famous for parking lots . . .

Where the air-pollution in Westmount is not excessive
Where unemployment follows overtime
and layoff precedes holiday . . .

Where newspaper literacy is high
Where poetry doesn't sell

City of bop churches and modern bars
Home of the Montrealer magazine
Emporium of Pinky Stamps and the give-away trade
Teenage harem of NDG (in summer shorts)
Boy nursery (in rags) of St. Henri
Old People's home of Westmount (in tweeds)

You've got marble piles (people kneel in your banks)
You've got the Hydra
You've got leaking gas

You've been sold down the Seaway
You've been had, Montreal! They've shot up your City Center
        —the American way!

Montreal, where's Stanley street?
Montreal, where's my house?
Montreal, where's the red light district I used to know?
Where are your great traditions? where are your historical
        sites?

Your plaques are rusting!
You don't even know where to dig for Hochelaga!
You've left the Indians in the slum of Caughnawaga
        while you go walking in furs!
You're all blown up inside!

Goodbye! Screw you, Miss Montreal!
Mange les patates frites! Go chez Eaton!

I'm moving to Ste-Agathe where I don't have to look at you
        anymore
                all through the summer
                        (in Montreal, summer is three weeks in July).

Louis Dudek

Montreal

Tender, sweet and eloquent, all the words for her. My burning unrest. Each day, her image renewed, her body more beautiful than the day before. I say more beautiful. I love this city, I love this woman.

Every season beautifies the house of our loves. Snow or sun, elusive spring, idle autumn. I will never know her body enough, I will never love her heart enough.

Each day I remove her magnificent garments and stretch out beside her in ecstasy.

Jean-Guy Pilon

Translated from the French by Bernard Lecerf

Hating the City

1
Walking the streets
I saw men fearful
gibbering behind
blank faces;
saw living hands and eyes
viced
in a complicated scream
of metal;
I saw men sick
with anger, sick with
envy, sick with
machinery;
jabbering chromium masks;
I saw dead slaves
shackle their children's children's limbs
to the piston-rods
of avarice;
I saw black shadows
vague forms in nighttime perspectives
of doubt;
I stared up
at paper pinnacles;
I saw
    ashen faces
hurtling towards me like purgatorial sleet.

2
Hating the city, I myself began to change:
my laugh
had an edge now.
The wryback, the amputee on six-inch
wooden stumps, yielded
new, perverse humors.

Trees were unreal
but at night
real cop-cars screamed.
My mind became
a machine of revenge
shaking itself to bits.
My flesh
striated
to bullets.

With a very strange smile
I heard men talk of God amid churchly
money-clink;
I saw men who might have been intellectual heroes
play panel games to profit hucksters.

I saw the campus poets
sipping critical tea from chinese cups
dreaming guggenheims
as their flesh
crumbled.
(They told me of "tenure"
      and of
            "point of view."   )

Yet always I saw the brief, zesty flame-burst of spirit:
a child holding its ear in the cold and laughing;
the disorganized mind leaping at a truth.
And the flame-bursts of jubilation:
      the after-hours
      jazzman
the one-night stand.

(and always the flame extinguished:
    the hurried departure with a quick glance
    over the shoulder:
    always the fuzz-fear.   )

Walking the streets I heard
foundations crack.

I saw buildings go down

before they were built

Bryan McCarthy

Love of the City

After a week of wandering through the world
Eating wherever we could, sleeping, washing ourselves
Wherever we could, in bars and railway rooms,
We came to this great city. Nothing
Will persuade us ever to leave it again.

The city loves us now it's moved us in:
The yellow sky comes down and fills the room;
Dirt on the floor is kind, the walls are kind,
Everyone's kind to us wherever we go.

And truly when death comes where will he find
A better room than here, better arrangements,
More courtesy, more eager friendliness
Than in this excellent street-scattered city,
This home, this network, this great roof of pity?

George Johnston

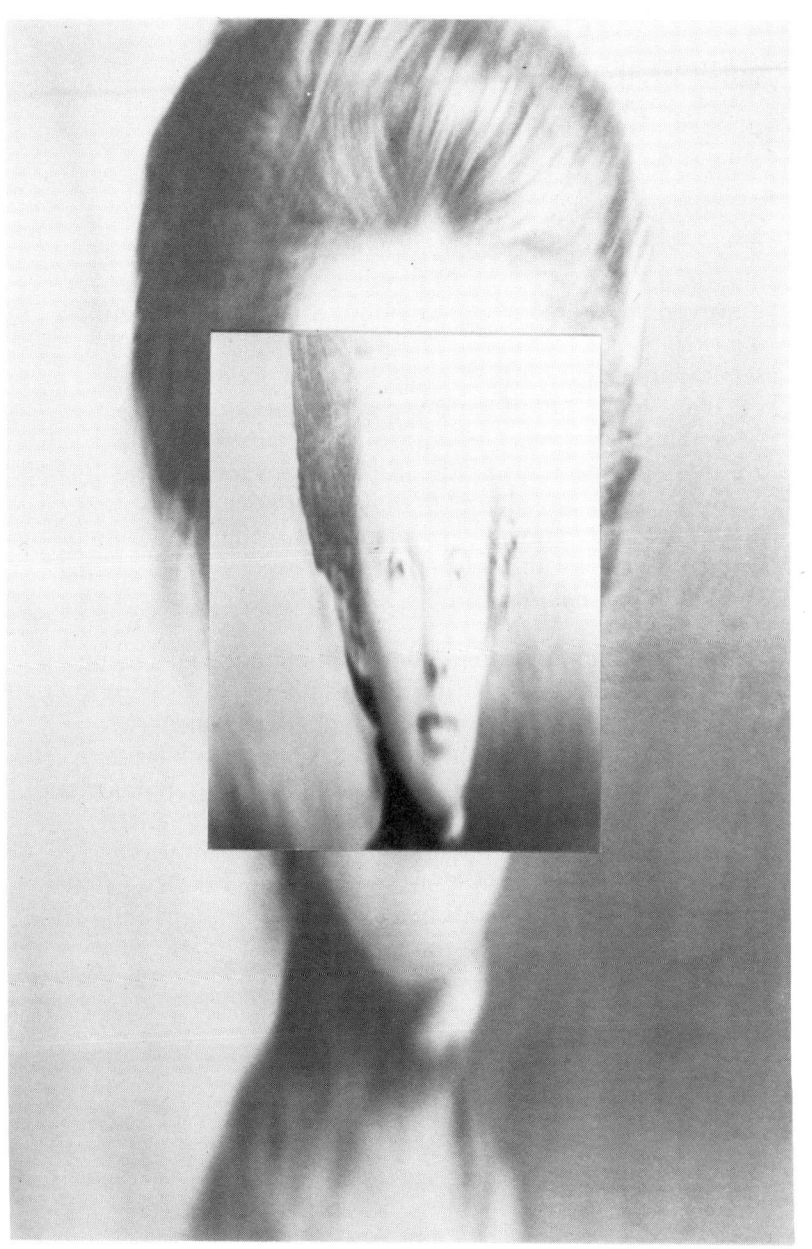

4

living on the edges:

poems about alienation

Alienation is not necessarily limited to city life and
relationships among different people; one can, for example,
be estranged from nature or from God. In this section,
however, the theme of alienation invariably exists in terms
of one person's relationship to another or others. The
separation takes different forms. In these poems, the
speakers, often intentionally vague in their outlines in order
to emphasize their lack of human contact, drift numbly
around the perimeters of life, isolated from society, friends,
or lovers. Or, in several cases, they experience that most
intense and terrifying kind of alienation — the "no-kidding
kind of alone," as Bill Howell ironically expresses it — which
involves being cut off from one's self.

More often than not, the reasons for the individual's being
alienated are not given; instead, the situation just seems to
be. But if the situation remains undefined, the imagery
in the poems is recurrent and unmistakable: blank faces,
claustrophobic rooms and, above all, night, darkness, and
silence. These are bleak poems, shot through with anxiety
and distress, fear and despair. And they are pessimistic
poems. Only rarely, as in John Newlove's poem, do we find
that one's alienation results in a renewal of strength and
the resolution that one — somehow — must go on.

Words

When we lie together as leaves enfolded
our words are sharply beautiful,
wounding as memory
holding us, shaken,
in an amazing dream

no longer together
our words
lie like tears

and your hand
passes like a comet
touching my dark with its radiance

Such leafing space between your eye and mine!

André Major

Translated from the French by G. V. Downes

These Are Yours

1
Because I want to see your face,
I feel sick.

2
A sheet you lay on . . . well,
it's been washed since.

3
The snow sings
to the swaying trees.

Children do
their Indian imitations
indoors.

Dry yellow tobacco
drops to the floor.

4
Haven't got

much left

now.

5
But still,
polished words. . . .

Shiny remnants
of our future dreams. . . .

6
Here you touched me.
In this corner we kissed.

7
It's as if
I had a talent for being hurt.

8
Alone at night
(in our deserted

beautiful country
in which

only the trees seem alive). . . .

9
These are your tears,
rubbed off on me.

10
My time is past;
but still I must continue.

John Newlove

The Closed Room

Who then brought me here?
There was certainly someone
Who prompted my steps.
But when did that happen?
With the complicity of what quiet friend?
The deep approval of what long night?

Who was it laid out the room?
In what calm moment
Was the low ceiling thought of
The small green table and the tiny knife
The bed of black wood
And all the bloom of the fire
With its red billowing skirts
Around its core enclosed and held fast
Under the orange and blue flames?

Who then took the exact measure
Of the trembling cross of my outstretched arms?
The four cardinal points
Start at my fingertips
If I turn myself round
Four times
For as long as will last the memory
Of day and of night.

When my heart was placed on the table
Who then laid the cover so carefully
Sharpened the little knife
Without any torment
Or hurry?

My flesh is bewildered and wastes away
Without this familiar guest
Torn from between its ribs.
The bright color of blood
Seals the hollow vault
And my hands folded
Over this devastated space
Grow cold and fascinated with emptiness.

Anne Hébert

Translated from the French by F. R. Scott

Wider than Clouds

Wider than clouds and more serene,
Higher than mountains and more sheer,
Night on the evening's sombre green
Angels of my despair appear.

These constant overshadowers
Who blur the sun with towering heads
Are my peculiar foes and followers
And are more true and older than all friends.

Clasped in the darkness of their misty wings
Lies all my life, the journey and the clock,
Under their snowy breasts my raven sings
And in their fleshless hands my visions break.

Unto the end I know their august flight
Will follow all my steps, the streets and hills
Of love, the sorrow and delight,
Till their wings cover me as evening falls.

George Woodcock

Loneliness of the Unemployed

One morning I wake up and my manhood is gone.
I cannot believe it. Then, faintly
I hear it crying. Thin muffled peeps
from the eyeless mouth. I tear out of bed
and begin to search,
turning over books and clothes.
After a frantic minute, I discover the thing
alone in my billfold on a chair.

It is lonely without the body.
I look at the hands and they do not say anything.
They cannot tell me what they are for.
Also the feet. The chest and stomach
can breathe and be hungry
but neither can say a word.
Food is embarrassed. Rice on my fork
looks the other way when it is brought to my mouth.

Once I woke in the night
and heard the body talking.
It spoke of its shame. It told itself
it was going away.
I broke in, to try to explain.
Silence.
We rolled back to back and pretended to sleep.

I stop a man on the street and begin to discuss myself.
He interrupts to assure me my situation is not my fault.
"But when you are poor you should not be in love,
have children, enjoy yourself," he tells me.
"These things are for people with money."
I want to thank him
but he has begun an argument with his newspaper.
The printer's ink is quite abusive,
wrangling and hooting over a detail.

Once I had a trade as a writer
but I left because I did not want to lie.
I became a teacher, and taught lies.
At last I just talked, but the language
knew I was lying. The words
ran out of my mouth and told everyone
what a fraud I am.
It is lonely without even words.
There are no women without money.
But even without money, I do not want to stop being a man.
I cannot even stop being lonely.

Tom Wayman

Evening Trainstation Before Departure

It seems I am always
moving

(and behind me the lady
slumped in darkness
on a wooden bench
in the park, thinking
of nothing: the screams
of the children
going down the slide
behind her, topple her mind
into deep trenches)

moving

(and in front of me the man
standing in a white room
three flights up, a razor
(or is the evening
a razor) poised in his hand
considering
what it is for)

move with me.

Here I am in
a pause in space
hunched on the edge
of a tense suitcase
(in which there is a gathering
of soiled clothing, plastic bottles,
scissors, barbed wire
and a lady
and a man)

In a minute everything will begin
to move: the man
will tumble from the room, the lady
will take the razor in her black-gloved hand
and I will get on the train
and move elsewhere once more.

At the last station
under the electric clock
there was a poster: Where?
part of some obscure campaign;

at this one there is a loudspeaker
that calls the names and places
(the sounds like static; the silences
thin as razorblades between)

at the next one there will be
a lady and a man,
some other face or evidence
to add to the
collection in my suitcase.

The world is turning
me into evening.

I'm almost ready:
this time it will be far.

I move
and live on the edges
(what edges)
I live
on all the edges there are.

Margaret Atwood

Foreigner

Between strange walls
you, foreigner, walk in silence,
sheltered from eyes
by the shady hands of fear
and the suddenly dropped
blinds of embarrassment.

A room will hold you a smile
but you will not look.
From a long past of walking you have come
wearing blinkers and the balanced book.
Now pressed in a corner by words
you have no face
and cry for love
in the leaning tower of self.

P. K. Page

Idiot's Song

Give me peace from you
allow me to go on
and be what I was before you
if there was ever that time

But talk to me talk to me
or die soon before I do
I'll come where your body is
tho it answers me nothing

But don't die
stay with me in the same world
or I'm lost and desolate
for here the light and dark
that touches you   touches   me
that you are here at all
delays my own death
an instant longer

Al Purdy

Night Fear

I do not know
If I really love you
Or if what I want
In your arms
Is just protection
Against the dark, against space,
The wide, lonely world
Outside.
It is as though I walked
A child
Shivering
Down a dark hall
Into my parents' bedroom
To find shelter again
In warmth of bodies
And the smell of human sweat.
I could not sleep
In my own empty room
Because it was so full
Of night.
I am frightened of the dark.
Hold me.

Elizabeth Brewster

Night Ward — New Year's Eve

There's a party downstairs tonight
and you won't go.   Lying back,
you recall the face of some distant
lover, celebrate at nine
without a pill.

The whole ward may go to sleep tonight
but not you.   If you close your eyes
something lonely may creep in.

On the other side of the glass
someone has taken away your things.
Maybe it's the locked door that
keeps you out but you suspect
it's something else.
Someone has chiselled bars
for the windows, there is no way
to ease yourself out.
In the stale air you hear
caged birds
plotting their death
like committed things
begin to do.

The room rotates in your hand
like a coin.   No visitors ever come
and besides
it's January now
or September
and the weather is never very good.
Old suicides leave
with tennis shoes
and second thoughts.   They'll never
remember you anymore.

In the hospital where you live
there are rows and rows of lavatories —
sometimes late at night you can go
from one to the other
and pull the chains.

Susan Musgrave

Alone Poem

Even with all the lights on,
I'm alone.
               Alone with myself.
Not the kind of alone
when all you've got to do is get up
and go, go out in the hall and holler
for the love who's always there, so
it's really safe, after all, to lie
on your back in the dark and wiggle
your toes under the blankets.
                                   No
this kind is the kind that starts you
wondering if maybe this is the way
you've always been, a no-kidding
kind of alone.
               There's no
such thing as "present," after all,
where you're the only one here.
                          You're so
alone you don't know who you are.
                           There's no
one to holler to, now.
                   Are you reading
this poem because you're alone?
                         I'm writing
it because I am.
               Can anybody write
a poem in the dark?

Bill Howell

Someone Who Used to Have Someone

There used to be someone
to whom I could say do you
love me and be sure that the
answer would always be yes;
there used to be someone to
whom I could telephone and
be sure when the operator
said do you accept the charges
the answer would always be yes;
but now there is no one to ask
no one to telephone from the
strangeness of cities in the
lateness of nightness now there
is no one always now no one
no someone no never at all.

Can you imagine what it is
like to live in a world where
there is no one now always no
no one and never some someone to ask do you love me and
be sure that the answer would
always be yes? I live in a world
where only the billboards are
always   they're twenty feet tall
and they circle the city they
coax and caress me they heat
me and cool me they promise and
plead me with color and comfort:
*you can get to sleep with me
tonight*/(the me being ovaltine)
but who wants to get to sleep
with a cup of ovaltine what
kind of sleep is that for someone who used to have someone
to ask do you love me and
be sure that the answer
would always be yes?

Miriam Waddington

5
the progress of barbarism:
poems of satire and social criticism

Satire seems to take root and flourish when cultural mores
are strong enough to encourage widespread assent, yet not
so strong as to command absolute conformity — a fair
enough description of Canadian society at the present time.
At any rate, the Canadian writer does not have to look very
far to find legitimate targets for his darts of criticism.

In general, modern satire spares the individual and follows
the rule of the eighteenth-century essayist, Joseph Addison:
to "pass over a single foe to charge whole armies." The
poems in this section, then, criticize and protest, and they
do so in a variety of tones of voice. At one extreme, Henry
Beissel complains bitterly about the horrors of war, Tom
Wayman about the violation of our ecological balance, and
bill bissett about intractable legislation. Less severely, John
Newlove takes to task the ritual of marriage, and F. R. Scott
ironically objects to the shortcomings of our educational
system. And at the other extreme, Eloi de Grandmont
humorously twists the foibles of parents, while Al Purdy
wryly comments on the threat of the United States to
Canada's identity.

The Ecology of Place

for Paul Bryant and Benton MacKaye

The place begins with water.
Lake, inlet or river
eddies into a clearing, turns
to planks and houses, businesses.
The forests go elsewhere.

The water moves the earth: supply
for the Interior and wealth
from the bush country.
There is a read-out of names.
Distant law begins to stop
the geography. A mountain is cut
by a noun.

But the place is a stone.
Magnet City. Farmboy and woman arrive,
immigrant. Mills, mines, speculations
become power somewhere as the Magnet turns.

There is a startup of railroad, and thruway.
The air fills; the harbor is
crushed rock; the creek solidifies
below the foodboard plant.
Oolichan, the candle fish,
go nowhere to breed.
But the nights are bright. California arrives.

　　　Then the City alone
　　　without the forest
　　　flows back looking for the child,
　　　free of beginning things, of logic.
　　　It wants to create again
　　　wilderness, but the trails are marked
　　　for power toboggans, no hunting.

It desires a countryside
but the cows stand in feedlots of
urine and dung, eating grain.
Hens turn endlessly in the tiers
rotating like huge trademarks of the corporations.

The City dreams of a balance.
Of finding land under its feet.
Of exchanging commodities that are not on fire.
But it is the dollar and oil who stay awake all night
to draw up the Plan. Fish offshore
begin to cough.

I walk into the street.

Tom Wayman

The Trappers

The trappers, trapped
between the steel jaws of their answerless
dilemma, their location,
follow, stop, stare down
at dead eyes
                caught in fur

Each time there is a repetition
of red on white, the footprints, the inevitable
blood. The dead thing, the
almost-dead that must be

bludgeoned, the few they leave
alive to breed for next year's
traps. The chain, the
steel circles

The snow snaps in their faces;
the forest closes
behind them like a throat.
The branches have
cold blood

    Their following, the abstract hunger
    to trap and smash
    the creature, to crush
    the red sun at the centre

also the wish
to mark the snow with feral
knowledge, to enter the narrow
resonant skull, to make each
tree and season an owned
territory

    but then the recurring fear
    of warm fur, the puritan
    shunning of all summer

I can understand

the guilt they feel because
they are not animals

the guilt they feel
because they are

Margaret Atwood

Transcontinental

Crawling across this sometime garden
now in our chaircars like clever nits
in a plush caterpillar should we take time
to glance from our dazzle of folders
and behold this great green girl grown sick
with man   sick with the likes of us?

Toes mottled long ago by soak of seaports
ankles rashed with stubble
belly papulous with stumps?
And should we note where maggoting miners
still bore her bones to feed our crawling host
or consider the scars across her breasts
the scum of tugs upon her lakeblue eyes
the clogging logs within her blood —
in the doze between our magazines?

For certainly she is ill   her skin
is creased with our coming and going
and we trail in her face the dark breath of her dooming

It is true she is too big and strong to die
of this disease but she grows quickly old
this lady   old with us —
nor have we any antibodies for her aid
except our own.

Earle Birney

The Admiral Hotel

Until I attended my friend's
wedding reception I was unaware
of the progress of barbarism.

Tense and uneasy guests
tried to avoid any reference
to sex, the wedding cake

was carefully plastered white,
the bachelors arriving in nervous homage
groaned for the longed-for punch,

female relations assured themselves
that the whispers were friendly,
free from the desk-clerk's bawdy

insinuations and the standard
jokes. They moved stiffly,
congratulating each other

in soprano hysteria, one glove off
and one glove on, their long-
tendoned hands groped for shoulders

and squeezed the muscles
of each other's upper arms,
or the upper margin brachio-radialis.

Speeches were made concerning
culture (we are all cultured)
and suitability, love

was also mentioned. The best man
looked madly about in terror
and wished for his bottle of rye

before reading telegrams
from the unpronouncable towns of Wales.
The groom became anxious for his sanity.

And I looked slyly about, glad
I had left my glasses home,
noting the general faith

and hope that everything
would be alright, if
not in this place,

at least when adjustments
had been made, desperately
sneering and quickly becoming

one of them,
while at the other end
of the room the fat photographer

carefully recorded the objects
of all the ritual.

John Newlove

Good Tidings and Goodwill in a Monsoon Drizzle

To everything there is a season
and a time to every purpose
under the heaven:
      boy and girl hand in hand
      holding a mekong dawn
      delicate in their hearts
a time to love a time to kill
      youth between rice paddies their dreams
      cut down ripped open their groins
      by bullets by machine guns by boys
      who left their girls their mothers
      spell bingo for a bang gang man's game
I have no words to express the satisfaction and gratitude I feel
for what you have done
      250000 children killed (& more to come)
stand to attention jesus the cardinal is coming
jingle jingle all the 11000 mile way
from the united states of paradise
      3000 boys faithful in a monsoon drizzle
      390000 santaclaus fans (& more to come)
      worship the lord of love and peace
with tanks planes rockets rifles gas
from good christian manufacturers
his eminence personally a shareholder
godliness is profitable to all things
      blessed who die for the lord
taking cocktails at the u.s. embassy
vice marshal ky fresh from an execution
the cardinal stale with t-bone steak
exchanging pleasantries about hitler
      refugees in the mountains a million
      dying from cold disease malnutrition
burp by saint francis burps the prince
the steak rare chitchat at saigon
modernize the gospels according to saint johnson
I came not to send peace but
      napalm poison chemical bombs

unto him that pierces thy cheeks offer also
        the hands pierced wired through cheeks
        pierced prisoners vietcong suspects
        all humans not u.s. are suspect
        crush balls bones slit eyeballs
        it's in the book: no flesh should glory
I say unto you love your enemies
        back in the states — 390000 g.i.s
        learning their bible lessons:
chapter and verse for every occasion
francis calls for war for peace paul
hatemercywrathlovehell to please all
great things doeth the lord which we cannot comprehend
        a village hewn out of the jungle
        by generations now defoliated
        flies red fever ants leprosy fear
        sweltering in huts hungerblown
        children bellies men and women
        tending scorched fields bearing terror
let the sliteyed bastards have it
buddhist atheist commies pour in
shells slugs liquid fire blessed
who are chosen from nazareth (texas)
from bethlehem (maryland) called to cast out
        the yellow heathen vermin roll in
        their own guts vomit peace lung &
        stomach freedom torn limb to limb
you are in defence protection & salvation of civilization itself
        pools of bloodmenwomenscreamchildrenfire
napalm once in contact with human skin burns the flesh to
the bone
        rockefeller research at the university of
suffer little children:
for such is the kingdom of heaven
        B 52 bombers fighters strafing schools
        highways open markets bombing hospitals
I have no words to express the satisfaction and gratitude I feel
for what you have done
        the mangled the crippled the tortured
        the love of many shall wax cold
in the name of the father (on wallstreet)

and of the son (in the vatican)
and of the holy pentagon ghost

Henry Beissel

Homo Canadensis

I didn't know him
    but thought somebody else did,
for everyone was friendly in that bar
    except this guy in the red checked shirt:
he was aggressive and pro-Canadian,
stubbing a Players outside the ashtray,
swaying in his chair and gulping beer
like water
    drunk and getting drunker—
"Best beer in the world," he said.
"Bout the only thing left that's really Canadian."
    And glared at us.
"Did you know 60% of Canadian industry
    is American owned?
They callem American shubshidyaries—"
Everyone laughed when he stumbled over the word,
and he slapped his hand hard on the table,
"Don't laugh!" he said.
"Okay, I been drinkin, I like to drink.
But don't laugh when you see this country
TAKEN OVER
    just sort of casually
like an afterthought, like a burp after dinner—"
    "So what?" somebody said.
"Everybody here knows we'll belong to the States
    in another 10 years . . ."
The guy swelled up like a sneering bullfrog,
"And guys like you deserve to be taken over.
But when you are you'll be 2nd class Americans,
like Negroes in the south, like Indians here—

You'll be 2nd class Americans because
you were never 1st class Canadians in the first place—"
Everybody stiffened.
                    "Okay," he said,
"I'll buy the beer and shut up."
But after a few seconds he couldn't keep quiet.
"Anybody ever hear of the San Juan Islands?
No, I guess not. Well, Canada got gypped there.
Anybody know about the Alaska Panhandle deal,
or remember the Herbert Norman case, by any chance?
Well, I'm tellin you, this country it being taken
like a glass of beer. It's a matter of economics.
And none of you guys really give a damn,
just slop your beer and wait to be taken
by some big bellied American in Washington.
And I'm tellin you, they're all greedy bastards—!"
"I like Americans," someone said mildly,
and it seemed just by chance his arm lifted,
meeting checked shirt's arm in the middle of the table.
That was all it needed:
"Okay, loud mouth, let's see you put me down!"
They call it "arm wrestling" some places:
and the yellow beer jiggled as clasped hands
pushed on elbow fulcrum—everyone watching.
The guy in the checked shirt was drunk
and the other guy more or less sober,
so it shouldn't have been much of a contest.
Their arms strained like two-thirds of a tripod,
and checked shirt put on the pressure,
"I'm tellin you they're bastards—!"
The other guy was big, but he collapsed quick,
knocking over a glass of beer and the salt shaker.
"Just shows you," checked shirt said,
looking around the table. He started to go.
"I gotta be gettin back. Be seein ya—"
"You been huntin?" somebody asked.
"That's right, up near Bancroft. Takin back a nice buck."
"Where ya from?"
Checked shirt grinned.
"New York," he said.   *Al Purdy*

82

Audacity

"Audacity is missing in Canada." The Times 30/11/59

They say we lack audacity, that we are middle class, without
the adventurousness that arises from the desperation of
the lower classes or the tradition of the upper classes.
They say we are more emphatically middling than any
country west of Switzerland, and that boldness and
experiment are far from our complacent thoughts.
But I say to you, they do not know where to look, and have
not the eyes to see.
For audacity is all around us,
Boldness sits in the highest places,
We are riddled with insolence.

Do you want audacity?
Let me tell you —
Any day in Montreal you may hear the guns crack at the
noon-hour, as the police give chase to the bank robbers
Who are helping themselves to the wealth of the land like the
French and the English before them, coureur de bois and
fur trader rolled into one;
You may watch the patrol-cars circle their beats to gather the
weekly pay-off from unlicensed cafés
Whose owners sell booze on the side to acquire the $15,000
they need for the $25 permit;
You may learn the name of the distinguished Legislative
Councillor who controls the caisse-electorale
Into which rattles the coin that makes possible the letting of
contracts,
And who tips his hat to the priest
And is saluted respectfully in return;
You may marvel at the boldness of promoters of oil and
natural gas, men too quick for production, fixers and
peddlers,
Getting their hands on concessions and rights, access to
underground treasures awaiting man's use in the womb
of our northland,

Playing the suckers and markets, turning their thousands to
    millions, loading the pipe-lines with overhead that is
    paid by the housewife who cooks her spaghetti,
Then solemnly demanding higher rates for sales of the
    product (extra hot, natural gas!) before friends on the
    Board of Control;
You may follow the hucksters and admen compiling their
    budgets, planning the assault on "public opinion,"
    setting the poll-questions,
Writing editorials for weeklies, letters to editors, telegrams
    to Senators, articles for journals,
Day after day on the job of confusing the issue, baiting the
    eggheads, laughing at the "culture kids" of CBC, fixing
    the give-aways,
Posing as democracy's friends and admirers, while under-
    mining the concept of government and welfare,
Singing the praises of free enterprise that relies on high
    tariffs, defence contracts and floor prices;
You may stand in awe at the audacity of journalists, twisting
    the news items by headline and rewrite, blanking out
    truth,
Ponderously laying down the conventional wisdom in un-
    conventional English,
While a few owners gather dailies into chains run by gangs
    of paid hack-men,
Then add on the radio stations and TV outlets, lest some
    glimmer of free opinion escape them;
You may be amazed at the boldness of churchmen and
    ministers, meeting in synod and conclave and conference
    to spy out our sinfulness,
Who wax indignant over lotteries, horse racing and the drink
    question, or, with Savonarola intensity,
Denounce crime comics and short bathing suits;
But all this is as nothing, not worthy of mention,
Beside the supreme, the breath-taking audacity
Of the great executives in their panelled boardrooms
Found at every point in the social structure where policy is
    laid down or decision taken,
Without whom no hospital can be opened, no charitable
    campaign launched, no church can engage a preacher
    and no university can build a building,

Daring to be omniscient, omnipotent, omnipresent, not to
    mention omnivorous —
These surely you can see in this Canada of ours, O London
    Times,
In this country that has the audacity to proclaim the
    "supremacy of God"
In its Bill of Rights?

F. R. Scott

The Launching

Any big event must have
the Ceremony of the Officials.

I had my officials picked out
long before starting to build
my master space rocket.
They included cabinet ministers,
arms makers, generals,
all the boys on the real inside.

When the Big Day came
they stood on a platform
at the foot of the monster
and made speeches
one after the other.

I let them talk
as long as they wanted to,
then, when the last one had finished,
I pushed back a little door
in the side of my brain-child
and invited them to enter.

When the last one had disappeared inside,
I closed the door, walked very deliberately
across to the control panel
and pushed a button.

Imagine my surprise
when it worked.

Raymond Souster

Examiner

The routine trickery of the examination
Baffles these hot and discouraged youths.
Driven by they know not what external pressure
They pour their hated self-analysis
Through the nib of confession, onto the accusatory page.

I, who have plotted their immediate downfall,
I am entrusted with the divine categories,
ABCD and the hell of E,
The pa. de of prize and the backdoor of pass.

In the tight silence
Standing by a green grass window
Watching the fertile earth graduate its sons
With more compassion—not commanding the shape
Of stem and stamen, bringing the trees to pass
By shift of sunlight and increase of rain,
For each seed the whole soil, for the inner life
The environment receptive and contributory—
I shudder at the narrow frames of our text-book schools
In which we plant our so various seedlings.

Each brick-walled barracks
Cut into numbered rooms, black-boarded,
Ties the venturing shoot to the master stick;
The screw-desk rows of lads and girls
Subdued in the shade of an adult—
Their acid subsoil—
Shape the new to the old in the ashen garden.

Shall we open the whole skylight of thought
To these tiptoe minds, bring them our frontier worlds
And the boundless uplands of art for their field of growth?
Or shall we pass them the chosen poems with the footnotes,
Ring the bell on their thoughts, period their play,
Make laws for averages and plans for means,
Print one history book for a whole province, and
Let ninety thousand reach page 10 by Tuesday?

As I gather the inadequate paper evidence, I hear
Across the neat campus lawn
The professional mowers drone, clipping the inch-high green.

F. R. Scott

Model Parents

There are parents who punish their children.
Others who scold them
Bother them
Badger them
Lecture them
Sicken them
Break them in
Cut them off
Keep them under and
Pull their ears.

Others who reason with them
Jaw them
Worry them
Confine them, bore
Them to death, chide

Them, chivy
Them, crush
Them, curse
Them and disinherit them.

There are also parents who chastise them.
Parents who pinch them
Strike them
Slap them
Spank them
Torment them
Knock them around
Smash them to bits
Hand them over to the Social Welfare and then
Go to bed and make others.

Then there are the ones who
Take away their dessert, keep them
From sleeping, forbid
Them to go out, cut off
Their pocket money, tell them to
Shut up.

Finally, there are those who give them
A good swift kick in the pants and a
Father's blessing on New Year's Day.

Eloi de Grandmont

Translated from the French by John Glassco

The Tolerant Philistine

If behind that toothpaste grin,
one eyeball one way, one the other,
sets an adding machine going tick-bang, click-clang;
if he'd amputate his mother's wedding-ring finger
for the price of a girly show:

tolerate it, brother,
tolerate it.
Realize he's human.

And this man makes his wife
a dunghill to crow on;
his "damn's," "you did's," and "you didn'ts,"
a fist-full of small flies
eternally at her eyelids:
tolerate it, brother,
tolerate it.
Realize he's human.

If it's all strictly for vultures,
a few smart operators, mere cheerful idiots,
and the rest living in a flaccid paroxysm;
its morals and LIFE editorials
a recitation for laughing hyenas:

tolerate it, brother,
tolerate it.
Realize they're human.

But if a poet grows a beard
and calls you a truthful name; if some pickets
hopped up on coffee and empty stomachs
squash a scab; if men's feet, pierced
and fixed with horseshoes,
kick:

never tolerate that!
Why, such tolerance could upset
your whole system of tolerance!

Milton Acorn

They Never Hurt No One but Yu Sure Have
Mister and Missus Right in Canada

LEGALIZE MARRAWANNA NOW
let yr children out of jail, sum
of them are in for up to seven years

liquor cigarettes and traffic
accidents are completely legal, tho
all proven medically harmful.

weed not addicting, dusint give
yu lung cancer, stunt yr growth,
wreck yr liver, cost as much as a car,

is this era's big deal crime. so all
th children of th
country, canada, 1971, see yu didint

think iud tell, are being busted, beaten,
lockd up, burnd, torturd cause these
can't fix up their

laws to follow even their own logic
can't follow even th advice of their own
doctors, lawyers, churchmen, seems

like maybe they'd rather kill their
children, cause these mothrs nd fathrs
can't decide whether to go on

living or blow it all up letting
mstr nixon make it alone to th moon
to die a serene not involved gasp

yu are all th children
ovr th moon yu kill
th venus powr

bill bissett

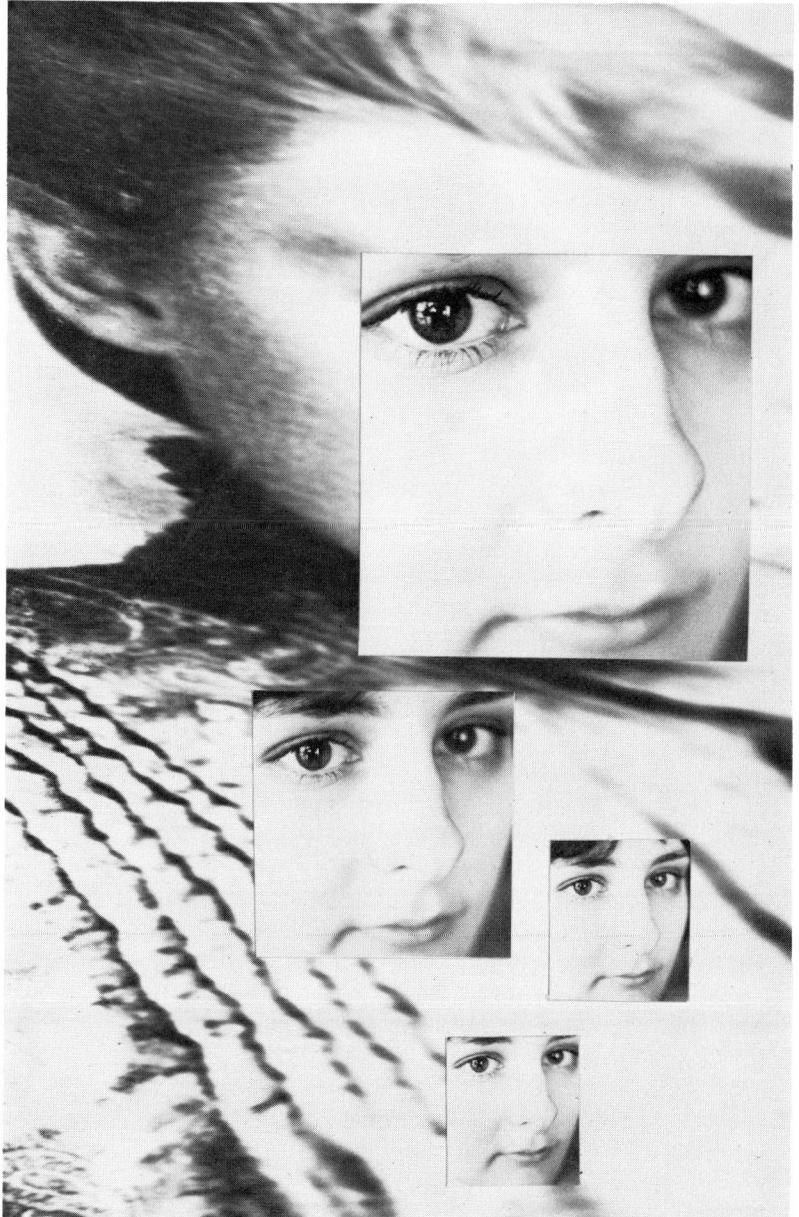

6
portraits:
poems about people

The poems in this section are about particular people. In many of the other poems in the anthology, the people are not fully developed individuals; they are generally used as vehicles to reveal attitudes, ideas, emotions, and states of mind. Consider, for example, Margaret Atwood's "Chronology," Bryan McCarthy's "Hating the City," or Anne Hébert's "The Closed Room," which appear in earlier sections. The speakers in these poems are somewhat indistinct in a physical sense; we come to know how they feel and what they think, but not how they look, where they are, or what they do. The reader may well regard them as "flat" characters. In the poems here, however, we get to know the characters more intimately; the poet zeroes in on the individual and gives us an extended and detailed image of the person's mental and physical life. "The Blind Man," "Letters & Other Worlds," and "The Stoker" — these poems give us "round" characterizations.

One of the most striking things about the people in these poems is the way in which they represent both the specific and the general, the particular and the typical. Most of the characters impress the reader as typical; we recognize that the lonely bachelor in Doug Fetherling's poem and the brassy streetwalker in Raymond Souster's poem could be *any* lonely bachelor or *any* brassy streetwalker. Yet at the same time, these people exist as unique individuals. The bachelor's overflowing ashtrays, his unused stove, his refrigerator that serves as a bookcase, the streetwalker's black hair, big smile, tight sweater, and sheer stockings — this accumulation of specific physical details establishes the person's distinctiveness in the mind of the reader. In the end, the poets in this section succeed in rendering that most difficult kind of portrait: the one that allows us to see that types are individuals and individuals types.

Bushed

He invented a rainbow but lightning struck it
shattered it into the lake-lap of a mountain
so big his mind slowed when he looked at it

Yet he built a shack on the shore
learned to roast porcupine belly and
wore the quills on his hatband

At first he was out with the dawn
whether it yellowed bright as wood-columbine
or was only a fuzzed moth in a flannel of storm
But he found the mountain was clearly alive
sent messages whizzing down every hot morning
boomed proclamations at noon and spread out
a white guard of goat
before falling asleep on its feet at sundown

When he tried his eyes on the lake   ospreys
would fall like valkyries
choosing the cut-throat
He took then to waiting
till the night smoke rose from the boil of the sunset

But the moon carved unknown totems
out of the lakeshore
owls in the beardusky woods derided him
moosehorned cedars circled his swamps and tossed
their antlers up to the stars
Then he knew   though the mountain slept   the winds
were shaping its peak to an arrowhead
poised

And now he could only
bar himself in and wait
for the great flint to come singing into his heart

Earle Birney

Prospector

Old man, you prospected summer
country of caves and gold.
With the rattlesnake and spider
you were a black widow without a mate
gone deep chrome yellow—
you shared with the sun
a babble of flowers and full
brown flawless centres where
you walked in a wilderness
of golden sleep.

Once I was a child
and saw you touch a mountain
wasp with your finger
tip to wing he didn't move
but shivered gently his petal shells
of yellow and black in the wide corner
of August. You watched solitary
wasps float down sunflower fields.

Old man, I dreamed you
wandered the mountains
in spring and planted
the hills with golden flowers.
When they found you
they said you were dead
but I knew that the wasps
had planted their eggs in you
and flowers were growing
out of your sleeping eyes.

Patrick Lane

Grandfather

Grandfather
        Jabez Harry Bowering
strode across the Canadian prairie
hacking down trees
               & building churches
delivering personal baptist sermons in them
leading Holy holy holy lord god almighty songs in them
red haired man squared off in the pulpit
reading Saul on the road to Damascus at them

Left home
        big walled Bristol town

at age eight
             to make a living
buried his stubby fingers in root snarled earth
for a suit of clothes & seven hundred gruelly meals a year
taking an anabaptist cane across the back every day
for four years till he was whipt out of England

Twelve years old
             & across the ocean alone
to apocalyptic Canada
             Ontario of bone bending labor
six years on the road to Damascus till his eyes were blinded
with the blast of Christ & he wandered west
to Brandon among wheat kings & heathen Saturday nights
young red haired Bristol boy shoveling coal
in the basement of Brandon college five in the morning

Then built his first wooden church & married
a sick girl who bore two live children & died
leaving several pitiful letters & the Manitoba night

He moved west with another wife & built children & churches
Saskatchewan Alberta British Columbia Holy holy holy
lord god almighty
             struck his labored bones with pain
& left him a postmaster prodding grandchildren with crutches
another dead wife & a glass bowl of photographs
& holy books unopened save the bible by the bed

Till he died the day before his eighty fifth birthday
in a Catholic hospital of sheets white as his hair

George Bowering

Letters & Other Worlds

*"for there was no more darkness for him and, no doubt
like Adam before the fall, he could see in the dark"*

My father's body was a globe of fear
His body was a town we never knew
He hid that he had been where we were going
His letters were a room he seldom lived in
In them the logic of his love could grow

My father's body was a town of fear
He was the only witness to its fear dance
He hid where he had been that we might lose him
His letters were a room his body scared

my father, jealous
at my mother's articulate emotion,
dove into the waters of the harbor
and swam after the ship waving farewell.
My mother pretending no affiliation
mingled with the crowd back to the hotel.

Once again he made the papers
though this time my mother
with a note to the editor
corrected the report—saying he was drunk
rather than broken hearted at the parting of friends.
The married couple received both editions
of *The Ceylon Times* when their ship reached Aden.

He came to death with his mind drowning.
On the last day he enclosed himself
in a room with two bottles of gin, later
fell the length of his body

so that brain blood moved
to new compartments
that never knew the wash of fluid
and he died in minutes of a new equilibrium.

His early life was a terrifying comedy
and my mother divorced him again and again.
He would rush into tunnels magnetized
by the white eye of trains
and once, gaining instant fame,
managed to stop a Perahara in Ceylon —
the whole procession of elephants dancers
local dignitaries — by falling
dead drunk onto the street.

As a semi-official, and semi-white at that,
the act was seen as a crucial
turning point in the Home Rule Movement
and led to Ceylon's independence in 1948.

(My mother had done her share too—
her driving so bad
she was stoned by villagers
whenever her car was recognized)

For 14 years of marriage
each of them claimed he or she
was the injured party.
Once on the Colombo docks
saying goodbye to a recently married couple

And then in his last years
he was the silent drinker,
the man who once a week
disappeared into his room with bottles
and stayed there until he was drunk
and until he was sober.

There speeches, head dreams, apologies,
the gentle letters, were composed.
With the clarity of architects
he would write of the row of blue flowers
his new wife had planted,
the plans for electricity in the house,
how my half-sister fell near a snake
and it had awakened and not touched her.
Letters in a clear hand of the most complete empathy
his heart widening and widening and widening
to all manner of change in his children and friends
while he himself edged
into the terrible acute hatred

of his own privacy
till he balanced and fell
the length of his body
the blood screaming in
the empty reservoir of bones
the blood searching in his head without metaphor

Michael Ondaatje

The Stoker

for Barry

They try to teach you things so fast in school
& if you can't learn that fast they fail you
but when you get out in the world
you don't have to be that fast,
you find things go slower.

I'm slow. That's my problem.
I can do anything but it takes me longer, that's all.

Used to be I could only eat certain things, no bread & so on
but now I can eat anything. They way I see it
it was all nerves. Whenever I got nervous my stomach
would act up, or whenever I got scared.

I got as far as Grade 6 & now they say I'm too old, at 18,
to be in Grade 6. I have to get three years
work experience before taking Adult Training.
They told me I'd never be able to work on an assembly line.
    They said
I didn't have the co-ordination. Can't move my hands fast
    enough.

I heard about this course at Mohawk College
where they teach you to move your arms faster
but when I phoned up to ask if I could take it
they said they were all filled up. They said
Don't call us, we'll call you.

I make $28 a week in the parking lot
& also I make $12 a week in my other job at the poolroom
filling the stoker. My mother's down in the dumps a lot lately.
She worries we don't have enough money.

She thinks I spend my money foolishly.
But with two jobs I make $40 a week,
that's not good but it's not bad.

To be a garbage man you have to have Grade 10.
Why should that be? That's just not right.
I may not have perfect co-ordination but you don't have to
       be able
to recite Shakespeare to throw garbage on to a truck.

I saw this advertisement for a radio announcer,
a free course. So I phoned them.
They said *Do you have a thousand dollars?*
I said I thought it was free. They said *Yes it's free
but you need a thousand dollars for books & equipment.
Besides that you need Grade 10.*
I said I only had Grade 6 & they said I'd be eligible
for the technician's course.
All I needed was $50.
My mother just said *Forget it!*

I want to get my chauffeur's licence
but no one in the family will teach me to drive.
They say I'm a risk.
I'll have to take lessons from a driving school but I can't
       afford it.
Anyway my mother says I'll be heart-broken
when I get my licence & find I can't afford a car.

I'm a good worker.
All the people I've worked for
say I'm reliable & competent.
Maybe I'm no good at reading & writing
but I'm good at arithmetic. And I've learned
to make change beautifully
since starting at the parking lot.

I want to have my own store some day.
I wanted to have my own grocery store
but I guess that idea went up in smoke.
There are already too many grocery stores in town.
Too much competition, everyone told me.

I really wanted to work in a grocery store.
I wanted to be a stock boy. But no,
you need Grade 10 & they said I'd run into trouble trying
to figure out what merchandise to put on what shelf.

Maybe I'll get my own bookstore.
My brother Clyde has a friend who has a bookstore in Toronto.
He gets these books—hardcovered—worth 4 or 5 dollars
that no one wants, they would just throw them in the fire.
He gets them & sells them for 50 cents. All profit!

But I want to be a salesman most of all. I can really talk.
They told me at Parkview Vocational I'd make a good salesman
so when I get my three years work experience over & done with
I'll be taking an adult training course in salesmanship.

David McFadden

Jamie

When Jamie was sixteen,
Suddenly he was deaf. There were no songs,
No voices any more.
He walked about stunned by the terrible silence.
Kicking a stick, rapping his knuckles on doors,
He felt a spell of silence all about him,
So loud it made a whirring in his ears.
People moved mouths without a sound escaping:
He shuddered at the straining of their throats.
And suddenly he watched them with suspicion,
Wondering if they were talking of his faults,
Were pitying him or seeing him with scorn.
He dived into their eyes and dragged up sneers,
And sauntering the streets, imagined laughter behind him.
Working at odd jobs, ploughing, picking potatoes,
Chopping trees in the lumber woods in winter,
He became accustomed to an aimless and lonely labor.
He was solitary and unloquacious as a stone,
And silence grew over him like moss on an old stump.
But sometimes, going to town,
He was sore with the hunger for company among the people,
And, getting drunk, would shout at them for friendship,
Laughing aloud in the streets.
He returned to the woods,
And dreaming at night of a shining cowboy heaven
Where guns crashed through his deafness, woke morose,
And chopped the necks of pine trees in his anger.

Elizabeth Brewster

Harry, 1967

Ol Harry just sits on the porch all day staring at himself and not seeing a damn thing.

Or to tell the truth he doesn't even sit on the porch. His house hasn't got a porch.

Or to tell the truth Harry hasn't got a house.

Harry lives in a ten-dollar a week light-housekeeping room and thinks of himself sitting on the porch of a house he never had.

Harry has become very familiar with oatmeal and macaroni in his old age. He is thirty-six, born in 1931.

Born after the First World War, born after the twenties, born just in time to barely remember a small portion of the Depression, born too young to fight in the Second World War, to remember details really well.

Harry is five foot seven and a half, Harry weighs one hundred and thirty pounds, Harry has dandruff, Harry has bad teeth and no prospect of ever getting them fixed, Harry wears glasses, Harry quit school at sixteen before he finished Grade Nine to get in on the big money.

Harry looks like he's had TB all his life but Harry hasn't, Harry has nothing and looks like getting less.

But Harry sits on that porch all day feeling the sunlight almost and not seeing a damn thing. It's been a lousy life and it's only just half over.

Harry is thirty-six and he doesn't even dream about women anymore. Harry knows he'll never touch a woman again.

So what's the use of thinking about it.

But Harry used to see things.

Harry went to Ethiopia and was a general in a revolution.

And he killed the Emperor with his own hand.

And his gallant tribesmen swept down upon the lines of khaki machinegunmen and sabred everyone of them.

Harry was nicked by a fragment of shell that left an inch-long cut like one a knife would make on his forearm.

And Harry had no expression on his face when he removed the cigarette from his mouth and used its burning tip to cauterize the wound while fat newspapermen gasped in admiration as the faint smell of toasted flesh reached them.

And the movie cameras whirred.

And Harry waved his sword and ordered his cavalry to charge and all around the world movie audiences watching the Movietone News gasped as Harry slaughtered the old Emperor himself and his admiring tribesmen crowned Harry king and Harry . . . .

Harry always thought the word was calvary not cavalry, legacy of a short time at Sunday School in the damp cloak-room of a prairie United Church.

That was a long time ago to Harry and he has a long time to go.

And Harry doesn't see anymore.

He doesn't know that it's useless to see things that can never happen, he doesn't know that for him dreaming is just a lie now, that seeing things is no good for him, too late: that isn't why Harry doesn't see.

Harry just can't anymore, that's all.

John Newlove

Outside Joe Beef's

In the salt surf of Montreal winter,
old whiskery mud cat. His fins are rumpled newspapers
swaying tattered from leaky pockets

Wary and wild as though in Lachine rapids,
my undulating friend who does not know me
noses up to the lure of a nickel or dime
dangled down from any sport's crooked finger

Somebody has gaffed my old friend mud cat already
The lining of his torn coat drags adrift,
a pulled-out wound, seaweedy

I have lost many friends in these brackish streets of years,
among our rotting harbor bones,
through wintry sludge of flesh

Mud cat, let me touch you
Do not be horrified at my torn-out face.
I look with you for a shining philosophy
that some vile sporting god may dangle down

R. G. Everson

Jeannette

Jeannette in a fight
calling in boy friends
to wreck a café,
Jeannette dead drunk
swinging at a cop,
Jeannette on the habit
riding it up
riding it down,

Jeannette in jail
and out again,
Jeannette on the corner
of Dundas and Jarvis
with the old reliable
merchandise for sale.

Some day they'll find her
with a knife in the chest,
or choked to death
by one sheer stocking:

but tonight she's the queen
of this crawling street,
Jeannette with her sweater tight,
proud to show them off
to all the boys:

black hair, big smile,
that's Jeannette.

Raymond Souster

A London Hermit Looks on the Bright Side

I have no telephone
I have no timepiece
I have no radio
I have no telly
And I do not read the papers for I have
no interest in rape

I learn about the weather when it happens
I go to the cinema rarely and only stay
for the adverts
But I sometimes take walks in the courtyard
or, less often, take out the rubbish

My sole contact with the world then
is the electricity meter I have come to adore
Jutting like an ear from the wall
where it's screwed, it breaks up the pattern
of all those fleurs-de-lys
With the unfaltering regularity
of Almighty unfaltering God, it clicks
off the kilowatt hours between one week
and another

It now reads oh-oh-sixty-nine
The postman came but left me nothing
at oh-oh-sixty-four
Minus five-five-seventeen was the year
the first Kennedy was shot
And though Rome fell before electricity
was known my new-found system can easily
pinpoint this or any reality at will

My bathtub has a ring indelible under torture
My ashtrays are like massacre sites high up
in the Andes
The gas is not connected so my stove sits
in its crate
and my fridge, unpacked but plugless,
serves better as a bookcase
Being as I am a bachelor I lack
a certain fulfilment in life
which my meter has supplied me
these long months under lamplight

Doug Fetherling

The Blind Man

for Werner Berg

He stands at the edge of the abyss
and digs his nails into the dark.
He hears the light
sing white-voiced
breath-taking in space.
He feels the joy in things.
But in the orbit of his eyes
pain wheels black and icy
about his periscian heart.
What is unknown
                    lies in ambush
on all unsounded sides.
Tensed, his fingers move
probe the void
                    assess the emptiness
in which all things are wrapped
and come upon the palpable
cold . . . hard . . . flat . . . smooth —
glass, window, mirror?
His fingertips stare
life obscurely in the face.
The next moment is yet
impenetrable at his feet.
Is this the abyss?
The echo of his steps
fathoms shadows
and charts his path
abrupt and refractive as batflight.
Every sound is a window
with its blind drawn.
He flings them open,
his fingers reach feel scratch
the surface of the dark
and find home
                    where
everything remains invisible
waiting for his touch

words come out to meet him
thoughts embrace him —
ghost companions
                    unseeing him
through the long night.
Always he is alone
alone with them
under the forbidding wings of his fate.

In the shadow of his fate
his reflections have eyes.
His hands are his mirror
holding the imprint
of his darkest hours.
The wind is a black-feathered fan
concealing all but the eyes,
cooling fire images on his cheeks.
Mocking the shadowplay of the sun
that rises on his brow
and sets in his dead retina.
Behind them
                    in the sombre skull
cold, hard, flat and smooth
fuse into lucid form,
feeling is transfigured
and what he hears and senses
turns into color —
everything here becomes light.
Here, in his solitary workshop
his hands are tool and vision
as he cuts the face of our world
into night's hard ebony.
Here, at the cerebral core of darkness
he knows the joy of creation
as on the first startled day.
Night remains starless outside.
The sun brushes his eyelids
                    soft
                    and
                    still —

Judaskiss of the eternal dark!
In the orbits of his eyes
frustration wheels and screams.
He lifts his head,
then runs his fingers
over the black keyboard of light
searching for the music
that comes to him from the abyss
bitter nocturne
that surrounds him
                    like a secret.

Henry Beissel

The Winemaker

for Alfred Purdy

the winemaker comes to Toronto
the urgent winemaker comes
        from a little rural cottage
comes to Toronto (can't stand the place, just
        passing through)
with fingers dyed a deep magenta from the stubborn grapes
with one foot on the pavement
and the other poised for flight—

the winemaker invades Toronto
and the city ignites under his heels
        and in a few hours he has accomplished
everything and condenses all possible
        appointments into urgent minutes wherein
the entire history of Canadian poetry
is brought up to date over tavern draught
        or that purple homemade stuff
that dyes the guts a deep magenta—

the winemaker comes to Toronto
    disguised as a dervish to chase himself
back and forth across the urgent purple city, a living query
of his own movement—like those poems of his that go
    round and round and where they stop nobody
guesses—
the winemaker comes to Toronto
(can't stand the place just passing through)
    and leaves a pile of urgent
poems in his wake and leaves again
    for the little rural cottage
back to the deep magenta twilight of Ameliasburg
to write those poems that turn and keep turning

                    (there isthe man. he returns,
                        he is always   returning)

Gwendolyn MacEwen

The Tramp

Dirtying the joy of the returning exile
At the hemlock lane falling from the crest,
He rises like conscience or the paternal call.

Lolling face, tufted by tangled waste,
Round as balloon painted with mouth and eyes,
Deflates a grin above a woollen chest.

Negroid lips split and eyes glitter two ways,
The paint becomes alive, like blood under dirt,
The rubber features vivify with menace,

And tell the story of the mountain chart
Fastened to the otherwise worthless will
And the search postponed by an unstable heart.

Then, promising gold from the eventual spoil,
Takes conscientious pence and limps downhill.

George Woodcock

7
kinds of loving:
poems about love

Perhaps the most recurrent theme in literature is that of love.
Love has many faces and many forms. One can, for
example, love God or nature or one's country. Or one can
love one's parents, family, or friends. In this section, however,
love is seen in one of its most important forms: love
between a man and a woman.

To define the nature and meaning of love is not an easy job:
George Johnston can only estimate that there are "seventy
times seven kinds of loving." The common factor present in
most of these poems, however, is that love is a necessary
thing if we are to live as fully human beings: not loving
or not being able to love is to live in a state of hell. Beyond
this, many of the the poems suggest that love is a kind of
island in a sea of uncertainty, a sanctuary where separate
selves may meet and meld. Sid Marty, André Major, Gilles
Hénault, and Jacques Brault all emphasize this aspect of the
love experience. At the same time, paradoxically, love is
seen as a fragile thing; it has to be handled with care. No
particular human relationship is constant or permanent, say
Dennis Lee and Dorothy Livesay; instead, it is as unstable
and unpredictable as the human beings who partake in it.
Many of these poets also celebrate the physical side of love;
Roland Giguère and Leonard Cohen, sensitively affirm that
sex is an integral part of love between a man and a woman.
All these things, then — these and more — amount to loving.

The Art of Loving

We have no choice, really, about love.
We are composites, all of us.
From Peter Sellers talking to himself
to Catherine declaring, "I *am* Heathcliff!"

Or think of Orpheus, if you've a mind,
descending into his own dark.
Breaking shadows.
To exalt a fragment
is false, however.   Look too hard
and you will lose what you cannot articulate.

Always we are seeking Persephone.   But she
becomes enamoured of her dusky Dis.
Always is a corridor of mirrors,
the turning of Lot's wife.

Be still, then.   Pray
for all your failed loves.   Pray
for courage with purpose,
for stillness with concern.

Others may wonder about God.   I do not care.
We are all God, if we are anything.
This is to say
nothing, of course.   Nonetheless

I have said
everything.   That is why
it does not matter if you heard me or not.

Tom Marshall

A Protracted Affair

Above the lintel where I live
I set your name in majuscule
girl of my joy   girl of my grief
my being twined and steeped in yours
under a new moon   sleepless hours
between the ordinary sheets
girl of love's opening gesture   girl
naked in the panting lists
girl of one time and of all
naked in the panting lists
girl of love's opening gesture   girl
between the ordinary sheets
under a new moon   sleepless hours
my being twined and steeped in yours
girl of my joy   girl of my grief
above the lintel where I live
I set you name in capital.

Roland Giguère

Translated from the French by Francis Sparshott

Finding A Woman

With a woman you begin
and find an end
within a limit that expands
taking your measure

A woman rocks you, vessel and home
not yours, your gift is only a birthright
your worth is not assured

Trying his limits, a man grows
to fit a vessel, his measure taken
within a limit that expands
to all of sea-room
rocking in the night

A woman you touch from the inside
touching of an oyster and a pearl
touching of your own skin
making sure she's really there
not you, but around you
Within the compass of waters
you must shine
and be home

Compression is the force
to carry the ocean
against your centre

hove to on blood
in an anchoring ground
It makes your measure
an element that is a harbor

a woman you live with
touching her, seeing her
for a place to sail the words
in senses
you can only trust to depth

Delights unfathomable
of the volatile medium

So many lifetimes
that can't be lived

so many lines cast out
cut adrift, returning
to the same waters

As willow wands bend for a well
is finding a woman
Losing, to be
deadwood
in a seachange

Leaving a woman
a loss of boundary
and finding a woman
an expansion, a surrender

Sid Marty

After Nightfall

leafy hands
hands   her heart's wealth
the woman shares
in her island's overthrow
when I fall like a storm
like a bird of prey

and the snow coming upon us
limb to limb
and the cold sheltering us
each in the other
like grass in the dew
fire in the log

such am I
o idolized world of your arms
of your lap
such am I
in the halcyon
of a perfect night
the sorrow of being man
is dust blown away in the burning
of my breath
my boundless desire
swelling to a single touch of yours

your island is my lair
what joy to return
after the fall of night
when midnight howls
in my veins

you know that nothing is as true
as pleasure
as the bird quivering
in the sullen country of your island

so by our own magic
we escape from winter
and its terrible loneliness
to dwell within this night
this shell of tawny summer

    I am lulled upon your thigh
and your tender wrist beats like a heart
against my throat

André Major

Translated from the French by John Glassco

You Exorcise Me

Put your hand on my brow
to let me still know a little what life is
as it unfolds its bloom.
Your hand covers death
Your eyes are the color of my happiness
Your smile

        the collapse of a heedless horizon
opens for me a pathway of living water
Your words flush from cover the wild horses
whose foam is mixed with the red rush of my blood
Put your hand on my brow
to let me still know what the word presence means

Islands the color of oranges and summer
I am ferried toward you in the ark of this trust
A hand throws the mooring lines
What matter whether the boat hook bumps the heart
I shall read your traces in the sand
Hand you people the world
and through you I know that now is not
      a fabric of illusion

that I could roll up in it and go to sleep
In a hammock hung out of time
with a still landscape around me.

Naked thoughts are swimming in your eyes
I recognize their shapes of seaweed and coral
Transparent as fish that are light-bearing and blind.
Hand new-webbed with rivers, liquid joy, vast
and ringing daylight, thin snow on the embers of time
You alone have this power

of thawing out absence
of shaping the contours of a rock-hard time
of bending light toward the planet where I flee
    to escape in the gyrations of unnecessary actions

Gilles Hénault

Translated from the French by Fred Cogswell

Love Poem

I will swallow your
eyes and leave only
pools of darkness.

I will take the words
from your mouth and leave
only lakes of stillness.

Attend to my miracle,
I am kissing your body
making it white as stone,

The pools and lakes
of your eyes and mouth,
the white stone

Of your body will
make a labyrinth
of fabled cities,

And a marbled palace
of many rooms where
the whole world

Will be glad to pay
admission to wander
through the many rooms,

To look at my
miracle pools and soft
monuments until

At last the whole world
will go to sleep happy
at eight o'clock

Under a soft white fleece.

Miriam Waddington

The Ugliest Woman

It seems noteworthy to record
that today I saw the ugliest woman
I've ever looked at in my life.

And you might have guessed it—
a man was holding her hand as lovers do,
in fact, looked the happiest one on King Street;

while tonight no doubt he'll climb
those bulging thighs, board that monstrous stomach,
he her Columbus, she his fabulous
new found land.

Raymond Souster

White and Black

Two o'clock. So I loved her, didn't I?
At three, I know, loving is shut for the night.
The girl with the comma scar begins to cry.
Nice calves she had, but hairy in the light.

Her green eyes swim forever in the sea
Of bed—three starry weeks. Dawn makes its blur.
Lucky for us the fire that burned through me
Missed my heart's wicker palace, where I keep her.

How ugly she was, ugly, an ugly frown!
And beautiful, poor little cavalier.
And drunk, oh drunk, o flesh, keep my gorge down!
And her child's laughter made my heart go queer.

Suicide, she thought, was the only way.
"Four slugs I need, I'll do the job with four."
The big black laughed an accomplice's hurrah
Over his empty glass. God, what a bore!

That comma mark on your forehead, never mind,
Your gritty powder makes it look okay,
And the stuff around your eyes turns us all blind.
Let's follow the mocking crowd is what I say.

Look at them through the window, how they run!
On the floor upstairs —you were fifteen years old then,
Now fifteen minutes later you look done.
Should we try again? Come on, sweet, let's try again.

It's not your eyes, whatever the drums may play,
That we praise you for, but the whiteness of your thigh.
Keep those slugs for a week from Sunday, eh?
But why did you thank me? I keep wondering why.

Sylvain Garneau

Translated from the French by George Johnston

When It Is Over

The low-light recedes, the records recede, skin
        empties. Under my eyes
your eyes recede, I brush your cheek you feel what
        touch what clumsy much-loved man
receding? Your body is full of listening,
        exquisite among its own
shockwaves.   So. What
        space are you going into?
Over & over, love, what other
        music? Your
eyelids will be here for
        centuries, do not come to.
But flicker, come deeper, let be—the jubilation
        eases through your
body.   So. What
        space have you gone into?

Slowly, love, beneath me
        your breathing returns.
Now it is over, the flesh and resonance that filled that
        other space do not come to and
try to tell me where, for it is over.
        But drowse off now; as the after-pleasure settles
gently into our lives, it is over and
        over, and over, and over, and over and over.

Dennis Lee

Moving Out

for Raymond Souster

Dismantling our house
the features of our love are gone
our feet grow loud
in a bare room
arms long to lean
in softness between sheets
but all the paraphernalia and props
are out of reach

I can only stretch
for your arms now
and find an upright bed
between your bones—
without the body of your house
I'd have no home.

Dorothy Livesay

The Stranger in My Memory

At last I saw her body
Caught up between the banks of a river
Like a bridge
That fades away
In the fall of a dream

Hardly a shadow
Less than a ripple
And the rose of her breasts
At the water's edge
Like the print of algae

I loved her in my memory

Jean-Guy Pilon

Translated from the French by H. Porter Abbott

Knowing

I have in my mouth the honey of your mouth and of my body
    in your body
O unknown country my beautiful stranger of this love I do
    not know the name of your arms
around my neck like a night full of regal women in this
    unknown country
No do not speak let the breath of your breath breathe on
    my lips
Do not speak stay with your moans wholly my sparrow my
    captive
and my silence is in your eyes as a strange body I am
    absorbed in the water of your eyes
I am lost and search and roam in the kernel of your hair
I disappear in you O sleep of man O house of love
I die in you I have no face but your face and look you are
    grieving to die in me
You no longer exist I no longer exist   we are come and as
    one to our newness

Jacques Brault

Translated from the French by F. R. Scott

You Have the Lovers

You have the lovers,
they are nameless, their histories only for each other,
and you have the room, the bed and the windows.
Pretend it is a ritual.
Unfurl the bed, bury the lovers, blacken the windows,
let them live in that house for a generation or two.
No one dares disturb them.
Visitors in the corridor tiptoe past the long closed door,
they listen for sounds, for a moan, for a song:
nothing is heard, not even breathing.
You know they are not dead,
you can feel the presence of their intense love.
Your children grow up, they leave you,
they have become soldiers and riders.
Your mate dies after a life of service.
Who knows you? Who remembers you?
But in your house a ritual is in progress:
it is not finished: it needs more people.
One day the door is opened to the lover's chamber.
The room has become a dense garden,
full of colors, smells, sounds you have never known.
The bed is smooth as a wafer of sunlight,
in the midst of the garden it stands alone.
In the bed the lovers, slowly and deliberately and silently,
perform the act of love.
Their eyes are closed,
as tightly as if heavy coins of flesh lay on them.
Their lips are bruised with new and old bruises.
Her hair and his beard are hopelessly tangled.
When he puts his mouth against her shoulder
she is uncertain whether her shoulder
has given or received the kiss.
All her flesh is like a mouth.
He carries his fingers along her waist
and feels his own waist caressed.
She holds him closer and his own arms tighten around her.
She kisses the hand beside her mouth.
It is his hand or her hand, it hardly matters,

there are so many more kisses.
You stand beside the bed, weeping with happiness,
you carefully peel away the sheets
from the slow-moving bodies.
Your eyes are filled with tears, you barely make out the
    lovers.
As you undress you sing out, and your voice is magnificent
because now you believe it is the first human voice
heard in that room.
The garments you let fall grow into vines.
You climb into bed and recover the flesh.
You close your eyes and allow them to be sewn shut.
You create an embrace and fall into it.
There is only one moment of pain or doubt
as you wonder how many multitudes are lying beside your
    body,
but a mouth kisses and a hand soothes the moment away.

Leonard Cohen

Listen to Me at Crowe Lake, My Love

1
To love is to listen;

and I am walking behind you in the wilderness,
you carrying the compass
and my trust

listen to me, my love,
as we leave the road
and go into the trackless bush
of the back lakes,
me walking behind you, obedient as a squaw,
saying as I look at your back,

There cannot be death
when you love someone this much!

2
And now you are going to leave me
here on this high oak ridge;
the land grows too rough for my going with you;
you say you will be back and I believe you
and let you go and lie down on the moss
and sleep in the sun under the reddening oaks
until your footstep falls on the fallen leaves
and you are standing above me saying,
"I could not find the lake; we will have to try again."

We laugh together
and re-name the lake Elusive Lake
and then you come down to me
saying, "Woman, woman"
and *Man,* I am with you

man I am with you,
near or far,
in this time or some other,
with or without rings,
bound simply by the mystery
of certainty,
faith come full circle
sight without seeing.

I kiss your face forever

I cannot imagine my life without you
nor, for that matter, my death

to love is to listen

listen to me at Crowe Lake, my love

3
The way of a man with a woman
and the way of a woman with a man

this is all we garner from our parents
and this is all we can give our children —
nothing else substitutes
and nothing else matters

and you and I shall only love each other
according to this inheritance,
and you and I shall only love each other
according to the pattern
(or the pattern-breaking)

to believe in someone later is to have been believed in
by someone earlier;
to trust is to have trusted so much
and to have been trusted so much
that one learned to trust oneself
and then the others;
to love is always to have been loved enough
for oneself
that one has learned how to love oneself
and then the others;
and how to commit oneself is to have perceived commitment

between the lines in childhood,
the steadiness maintained
underneath the unsteadiness

and you cannot love anyone later
if you have not been set free to love earlier;
to have once been freed is always to allow that freedom
to the others;
and to have been loved and then let go free is always
to be able to love and then let go free;
to have known a loving that is joyous
and growing and generative
is to give out all these things in your turn
to a loved one

to have stood in the presence of the yin and the yang,
to have known *that* as a child
is to accept nothing less in your own time
of choosing

the courage to love
comes from someone
who had the courage to love

I am listening to you at Crowe Lake, my love

tell me how it was with you
so that I may know how it will be with us

4
and I can tell you now that I love you so much
I would set you free tomorrow
if you should find someone else
who will make you happier than I
or, if you should so choose,
although I cannot make any promises

to love you beyond my lifetime,
within my life I can love you so much
that I will be able

to push back your death
with the hand
you now hold
in yours

at our beginning

5
"There cannot be death
when you love someone this much!"

There are three echoes in the woods
at Crowe Lake

my voice,

someone gone before us

and someone coming after

Joan Finnigan

Home-Made Beer

I was justly annoyed 10 years ago
in Vancouver: making beer in a crock
under the kitchen table when this
next door youngster playing with my own
kid managed to sit down in it and
emerged with one end malted—
With excessive moderation I yodelled
at him
      "Keep your ass out of my beer!"
      and the little monster fled—
Whereupon my wife appeared from the bathroom
where she had been brooding for days
over the injustice of being a woman and
attacked me with a broom—
With commendable savoir faire I broke
the broom across my knee (it hurt too) and
then she grabbed the breadknife and made
for me with fairly obvious intentions—
I tore open my shirt and told her calmly
with bared breast and a minimum of boredom
      "Go ahead! Strike! Go ahead!"
Icicles dropped from her fiery eyes as she
snarled
      "I wouldn't want to go to jail
        for killing a thing like you!"
I could see at once that she loved me
tho it was cleverly concealed—
For the next few weeks I had to distribute
the meals she prepared among neighboring
dogs because of the rat poison and
addressed her as Missus Borgia—
That was a long time ago and while
at the time I deplored her lack of
self control I find myself sentimental
about it now for it can never happen again—

Sept. 22, 1964:   P.S., I was wrong—

Al Purdy

The Married Man's Poem

Five years married
and he has never once
wished he dared kill her,

which means

they're happy enough.
But it isn't love.

Alden Nowlan

Veterans

There are seventy times seven kinds of loving
None quite right:
One is of making, one of arguing,
One of wheedling in the night
And all the others one can think of, none quite right.

Yet they are all good,
Paying attention, giving the low-down kiss;
Answering back in the heart is always good
And coming out of a sulk is almost bliss.

There is a kind of loving in grass and weeds,
One in brass beds, another in corridors;
An uncanny kind that turns away and bleeds
And a gorgeous kind, practised by saints and bores.

They are all hard,
All seventy times seven, hard as can be:
Veterans of loving are wary-eyed and scarred
And they see into everything they see.

George Johnston

8

the poem is for all things:

poems about poetry

In this section, the poems are about poetry and the making of poems. Often, when a poet writes a poem, the end product is not, strictly speaking, a personal and private thing. Instead, it represents an amalgam of the poet's observations, experience, and imagination. The speaker in the poem is often a *persona,* someone talking for the poet but not necessarily saying what the poet himself feels, thinks, or believes. In the poems that follow, however, the poets tend to drop their masks and speak to us more openly and directly; they tell us what they think, not what they think someone else thinks. What they tell us here concerns esthetics, the origins of poetry and the nature of the poetic process, the intention and meaning of poetry, the function of the poet, and other related matters.

Now all these statements can and will enlarge our understanding and deepen our appreciation of poetry in general; all of the poets here have the ability to speak and write critically about their own work. But at the same time, we must remember that when the poet assumes the role of the critic, he tends to make statements that are highly subjective and personal; accordingly, each of the poems that follow has something quite different to say about the nature of poetry and poets. Poems, J. Michael Yates tells us, must capture and contain the most elusive of thoughts: they "must speak of things / Which go quickly / Through shadows of consciousness." A poem must be moral, it must tell the truth, says Ralph Gustafson; while Dorothy Livesay argues that it is the sympathetic response of the reader that completes and gives meaning to the poem. Louis Dudek represents, in a humorous and ironic way, a point of view that is more prevalent than one might expect — that the poet is a faker and that poetry is "a lot of horseshit." And Walter Bauer points out that, in spite of society's neglect and even persecution of the poet, his voice will never die out permanently. In the end, though, we must keep in mind that the poem is not for one thing or another thing; it is for all things.

I Wonder How Many People in This City

I wonder how many people in this city
live in furnished rooms.
Late at night when I look out at the buildings
I swear I see a face In every window
looking back at me,
and when I turn away
I wonder how many go back to their desks
and write this down.

Leonard Cohen

I'm Not Alone . . .

I'm not alone and all is not done yet
Somewhere someone is born to take my place
As now my hand so fresh so tired above
The faded lustre of some verse delays

And still I would believe that I begin
And in my turn the universe would name
Yet see myself treading a vast desert
Where day declines with every step I gain

So much has happened on this scrap of star
Madmen bitten by flame to puff their rhyme
Their moment of song, epic, painting, in vain
Who putrify in the charnel house of time

Because I too with rare sounds want to voice
The rich boredom that deigns to live in me
And like a dismal miser want to spend
Mornings and evenings on this vanity

And all who come will trim their wicks again
And we shall relight this stubborn little lamp
Deep in their brains and not owning I am lost
I seek the word while still the ink is damp

Gilles Vigneault

Translated from the French by H. Porter Abbott

There's a Kind of Hush

The poem is for all things tonight
that are tender and alone:
the tiny kitten with curled paws asleep

on the bed, as I sit reading what
the students have used
to hide themselves:
the formula essay copied
to tell of a lost boyfriend,
the death of a father.
Lines to announce
I am not going to like
what they are about to say,
that they can't possibly explain what they feel.

Words written slowly at the desks
in the dormitories, nervous because
they are late, because they will not please.
Hunted out on the typewriter
between supper and math
or a date. Worried later.
Sweated. Alone. Ashamed.

The poem
is for myself, at two
in the morning, opening the refrigerator
in the quiet: how I came to have
these oranges, that celery,
the sandwiches.

And for all those frightened and lonely
dying tonight: in pain and in fire
or little by little
here and in Asia
that my coffee should be warm,
the lights burn, the pen move,
these hours be still
for the marking.

Tom Wayman

The Memory of a Poem

Out of the air I draw the memory of a bird.
Out of the earth I draw the memory of a tree.
From the memory of the bird
and the memory of the tree
I make the memory of a poem
that weighs lighter than air
and floats away without wind.

Michael Bullock

Poetic

It is dangerous
to think in a poem
and doubly so to dream

At night words grow
too big for the man
I know

Having strained my limbs
in quixotic attempts
to encompass them

Recount for yourself
those frantic apprehensions of
the vision in the glass of beer
myopic miscalculations
of rudimentary organs and

Other
natural
phenomena

Poems jumping from the tips
of my immature fingers

Reams of conjured testimony
falling in disorder
under my desk

Value
lives in the mind
of an economist.
Beware

Twisting metaphor
and hardening animal matter

The authentic dance
is the wobbly stance
of a living man

Lionel Kearns

Poem

It must speak of things
Which go quickly
Through shadows of consciousness
Like animals in the thicket
You cannot quite
Be sure you've seen.

J. Michael Yates

Esthetique

Good poems should rage like a fire
Burning all things, burning them with a great splendor.

One wrapt flame at noontide blends
The seer's inhuman stare, the seaweed's trance.

And poems that love the truth tell
All things have value being combustible.

Out of rubbish burning and burning comes
Mozartian ecstasy leaping with the flames.

Irving Layton

Poetry

Nothing can take its place. If I write "ostrich"
Those who have never seen the bird see it
With its head in the sand and its plumes fluffed with the wind
Like Mackenzie King talking on Freedom of Trade.

And if I write "holocaust," and "nightingales,"
I startle the insurance agents and the virgins
Who belong, by this alchemy, in the same category,
Since both are very worried about their premiums.

A rose and a rose are two roses; a rose is a rose is a rose.
Sometimes I have walked down a street marked No Outlet
Only to find that what was blocking my path
Was a railroad track roaring away to the west.

So I know it will survive. Not even the decline of reading
And the substitution of advertising for genuine pornography
Can crush the uprush of the mushrooming verb
Or drown the overtone of the noun on its own.

F. R. Scott

Where a Poem Departs From the Truth

Where a poem departs from the truth it is a bad
Poem. If I were to say this poem is moral
I mean it is hard as coins though the currency
May fluctuate, it is the weather in absolute
Zero, a cold fact, or a hot significance
It may be, a lighting of newspapers where no

Flame is, as at Solfatara where
If a man goes through the crust his leg melts.
I have seen this thing happen. Flame or ice
The poem is moral. But if I say this poem
Lies, then it is a bad poem since
A poem is more than a way of happening, it is a way
Of concluding, as the walls of the Sistine Chapel
Cannot do without Michelangelo: as
The boop of a tuba arouses the cat from an illusion
Of pheasants; or if I were to say this poem is owned
By a Jew with a Protocol for baptized children; this ruby
Has the utility of a hammer's head. You
Would reject this poem as a bad poem even
Though the music blow celestial trumpets,
The formal Alps show thunderheads of snow.

Ralph Gustafson

Poet and Critic

1

Words are so much more
than the thing seen, touched
(I argue with you)
they caress the jar
color its round belly
curl fingers round
its throat:
before the jar is tipped
words have us drinking from it.

2

Your poems sit
small gods upon my shelf
saying (you say)
only as much as form and shape
can shout:
but what I bring to them
is outside, stranger
than that spelled message
and what I seal
on the poem's mouth
is my tongue's pressure.

Dorothy Livesay

O Reader You

know
the poet is made of paper
can you hear him inside your eye
the scream of the tree
as you read him

know
the poem is a paper hero
who used to sing
when you prayed him

now
can you find him inside
your book of safety
matches can you feel

his burning can you heal
him when you strike

now
can you feel the dead tree
as you turn his pages away

Patrick Lane

They're Wonderful

But it's a lot of horseshit this
stuff of yours you call
poetry Why don't you guys talk straight
I know you're
fakers because
I've seen you and you look like fakers
You squeal and squirm if
somebody says christ this stuff stinks
All of you are
in the ashcan frankly You
haven't got a think to say to anybody
I've looked into your
chap—
books and frankly I am dis—
guested with
your la-de-da Why don't you guys make French pastry
Why don't you play chess It's just as good
for your speed Or why don't you get
yourself a piece instead of making these bits
I tell you fellas it isn't
worth it Your stuff is just
a joke You haven't got a thing I'm sorry

for you Really fellas I'm sorry
for you poets You get as pale as
macaroni reading and
writing doodads
when you're missing such a hell of a lot
You're missing a lifetime buddies
Come on out and have a glass of
beer and see
what there is to see Look at these bee-utiful
asses in the street
Try a hot dog Give it a lot of
relish And take off your glasses What
you like this eh It's noisy but
not so bad when they're changing
records Yeah
Now you're talking I can hear you
Go ahead and write
a poem They're wonderful
in bed too kiddo

Louis Dudek

The Thrushes Do Not Die Out

1
They have hunted down
The poet.
Yes, they have killed him,
The good-for-nothing, him
Who irritated everybody.
All the nine-to-five men,
All the dutiful housewives
They have disposed of him.

Yes, like a boy with a slingshot
Who shatters the flight of the thrush
And then, with a shrug,
Kicks
The dead songs into a ditch—
That's how they killed him.
They could not bear his singing
While they slaved
To pay off their mortgages
On the house, on the car,
On their lives.
Yes, they have killed him.
There he lies now in a ditch, now
Their world is exactly
The kind of world they want:
A godforsaken place, good
For making money, good
For growing fat and old without joy.
That's what they wanted, they have no
Regrets at all. They killed him
To get rid of him,
He disturbed them: he wasn't like them.

2
Later a scholar found
A bunch of manuscripts
In the ditch—that is to say
In a miserable room,
And he had them published
With his own assiduous annotations:
He had discovered a dead poet
Ignored by his contemporaries.
There you are, they said,
We always knew there was something
Something quite special in his voice.
Only, why wasn't he like us,

Regular, from nine to five?
He could've made a decent living.
The domestic animals said to the thrush:
Live without wings,
Fly without song.

3
Still later
They put up his statue
And the speaker,
A regular nine-to-five man,
Talked of the eternal
Poet.
Everyone felt elevated.

4
The time came
When no one any longer paid
Any attention to the statue.
Occasionally a thrush
Would settle on his shoulder
And sing into the dead ear
Of the poet.

5
Later still
A young man discovered
The dead poet's verses
And said, why did I
Not know him? He would've been
My friend,
Yes, he is my friend, I will
Follow in his footsteps, I will
Sing, I will
Not be a nine-to-five man.
Ah, my dead friend, he called,
You have lit up the world for me.

6
Then they started the hunt
All over again.
They will bring him down alright,
Yes, not to worry
They will kill him.
This, they say,
Is no placefor thrushes.

7
But the thrushes
Do not die out.

Walter Bauer

Translated from the German by Henry Beissel

9

withdrawing from the fire:

poems about old age and death

The poems here have to do with old age and death — the process of withdrawing from the fire of life. This section thus brings to full circle the various phases of life begun in the first section of the book with the poems about youth and growing up. In those poems we saw that young people lived life from the inside out; they saw themselves as subjects rather than as objects. But in these poems — especially those concerned with old age — the situation is reversed: old people tend to live their lives from the outside in; they often view themselves and their death with objectivity and detachment. A good example is Irving Layton's "very old woman," who calmly accepts the fact of her imminent death, knowing that she will "flame serenely" until its arrival and afterwards *shall be utterly gone.*

Death may come in different ways and at different times — sooner by accident or through disease, or later after the passing of time — as it does in these poems. In each instance, the poet uses the occasion to reflect upon and comment on the meaning of death and its relation to life. Dale Zieroth's "Father" is content to be old; he is no longer afraid, as he has been during life. P. K. Page's "Masqueraders," stripped of the "gold" of their youth, are, paradoxically, "shinier" in their old age. Elizabeth Brewster wonders if her old people watch their dwindling time with "hope, resignation, or despair." And the spectral characters in Louis Dudek's fantasy poem, knowing full well that death means nothingness, feel that they are "free" because life has meant only pain and fear to them. These reflections about old age and death, along with various others, are expressed in the poems that follow.

On Knowing Nothing

Others have seen men die
Or heard a woman scream
One last word *Never!*
How do I know the horror
That breaks the dream,
Hateful yet clung to
As the image hugs the mirror
With such a silver shiver
As chills and almost kills?

I know: but how or why
Out of this savory fatness I
Should suck the sharp surmise
That strangles dying eyes

I do not know. What have I done
To bring the Angel round my head
That I can smell his pinion
(Bond or wing?)
Whom I must hate and love?

The surgeon's jab, a woman's thigh
Give blank surcease
For short or long.
I cannot let the hollow
Interval alone,
But pick it like a scab
To probe the wound within—
As deep, as nothing, as the grave.

A. J. M. Smith

Obituaries

I look at obituaries

what interests me
are the figures
that tell me
the ages of the dead

If the ones I see
are less than mine
I am forced to stifle
a quick thrill of joy
at having outlived
a fellow human

If the number
I read is greater
I rejoice to think
of all the years
a man like me
may look forward to

but when the age
written there
is the same as my own
I shudder and wish
that there were no
obituaries

Fred Cogswell

The Clearing

Growing old is a withdrawing
    From the fire
In the little clearing
    Of desire.

It is moving to cooler
    Air on the fringe
Where trees are nearer
    And voices strange.

We need not shudder
    Or be afraid
Till we cross the border
    Of that dark wood.

Till in the dark glow
    Suddenly
We find the shadow
    Become the tree.

F. R. Scott

Father

Twice he took me in his hands and shook
me like a sheaf of wheat, the way a dog shakes
a snake, as if he meant to knock out my tongue
and grind it under his heel right there
on the kitchen floor. I never remembered
what he said or the warnings he gave; she
always told me afterwards, when he
had left and I had stopped my crying. I
was eleven that year and for seven more years
I watched his friends laughing and him
with his great hands rising and falling
with every laugh, smashing down on his knees
and making the noise of a tree when it cracks
in winter. Together they drank chokecherry
wine and talked of the dead friends and the
old times when they were young, and because
I never thought of getting old, their
youth was the first I knew of dying.

Sunday before church he would trim
his fingernails with the hunting knife
his East German cousins had sent, the same
knife he used for castrating pigs and
skinning deer: things that had nothing
to do with Sunday. Communion once
a month, a shave every third day, a
good chew of snuff, these were the things
that helped a man to stand in the sun for
eight hours a day, to sweat through each
cold hail storm without a word, to freeze
fingers and feet to cut wood in winter, to do
the work that bent his back a little more
each day down toward the ground.

Last Christmas, for the first time, he
gave presents, unwrapped and bought

with pension money. He drinks mostly coffee
now, sleeping late and shaving every day.
Even the hands have changed: white, soft,
unused hands. Still he seems content
to be this old, to be sleeping in the middle
of the afternoon with his mouth open as if there
is no further need for secrets, as if he is
no longer afraid to call his children fools
for finding different answers, different lives.

Dale Zieroth

Masqueraders

What curious masks we wear:
bald patches and gray hair
who once wore dark or fair.

Wear too much flesh or none—
a scrag of skin and bone.
The gold gone.

Bifocalled and watch-bound
who once, time out of mind
glimpsed world without end.

Worse masquerades to come:
white cane, black gaping tomb
as if we were blind, dead, lame

who, in reality, are
dark, fair and shinier
than the masks we wear or wore.

P. K. Page

Home for the Aged

The old men sit, five of them on a bench,
Half sleeping, half awake, dazed by the sun,
In the muted afternoon, between one broadcast ball game
    and the next.
Their thoughts are leaves that drift across a sky perpetually
    autumn.
Their hands are folded: they have done with the Sunday
    papers.

Decorously shabby, decently combed and clean,
They watch with half-closed eyes the passers-by,
The loitering lovers, the boys on bikes, the cars
Rushing eagerly to some scene of active life.

Their lives are folded up like the papers, and who can know
Whether their years passed sober and discreet,
With the measured, dutiful, regular click of a clock,
Or whether some old violence lingers still
In faded headlines on their dusty brains?
What boyhood do they wander in, what middle age forget?
And do they watch their dwindling stock of time
With hope, or resignation, or despair?

Elizabeth Brewster

To a Very Old Woman

Old woman, your face is a halo of praise
That excludes nothing, not even Death;
    I have looked upon your waxy and virginal torso
    And I see you now as a frail candle
Whose flame, the initial sputter of ignition over,
Burns gently and with composure.

So the first taste of death was bitter.
Now you burn with a composed glow
    Listening, half-amused like a superior person,
    To your bridegroom which is the Darkness
While each hour of your lovely embrace
Descends in ecstatic beads of silence.

Old woman,
What does he say, your bridegroom?

That his child, Death, grows in my womb.

What else, old woman?

That only my white and virginal skin
Seals off the darkness from the death within.

Old woman, with face ageless like snow,
What will you do now?

Flame serenely
Till like a warmed candle
I curve over
The arm of my hurrying bridegroom and lover

Is that all, old woman?

Yes . . .
No. When Death and Darkness embrace
Over me
I shall have no face
I shall be utterly gone.
Use the blackened wick
For a headstone.

Irving Layton

My Seven Deaths

When I was born the doctor said
to my father, "I think
we can save the mother,
but don't expect the child."

And I was born dead;

But the doctor
as some sort of experiment
or to add statitical data
to his paper on "Stubborn morbidity
in stillborns," maybe even
because I had an appealing quizzical look
on my face, the doctor
pounded me and flipped me in and out
of cold water and, after seven minutes,
straight from the collective unconscious

I gathered a bit of Old English
from Piers Plowman
and roared at the twentieth century.

When I was four I dabbled in death again;

I got Scarlet Fever
and, according the panic of those days,
was rushed to Isolation Hospital,
a Tender-Loving-Care-less place
of prunes and cascara;
once a week my parents could come
and wave to me through glass
and then they faded into another country;
from listening too intently
to my childhood deprivation,
Streptococci got into my ear;
the one-eyed ogre of a doctor came at me
with a midnight diagnosis,
"We must operate or it will hit the brain."
I screamed but they operated.
I think it hit the brain anyhow;
I have been writing poetry ever since.

And then there was the death of my First Love.

He said, "I've never loved you.
I just used you. Ha. Ha."
And I got out of the car ready to die
on the sidewalk but the next morning,
after hot cocoa and a good cry,
I was angry enough to go on with the lessons.

Death came to me one summer's dawn in an aeroplane;

Yes, I actually talked face to face with him —
he isn't a bad sort really,
ugly but very straightforward and honest
about his objectives —
and after he showed me the hand he was holding
I moved from a jabbering chattering idiocy of fear
into a peace I made with myself,
wrapped my life into epitaph,

> "Here lies Joan aged twenty-one;
> She intended to stay longer."

When we landed I looked like
a purgatory saint, benign,
composed, beatific, my hands
touching the air,
and walking such unexpected steps
upon the earth.

At the birth of my first son
the surgeon made the emergency slit
that saved two. And I awoke to red roses
and the little damp beat-up ball
in my arms. All-Eyes we called him
because he had seen his first death
at birth.

At thirty-eight
there was a drowning that almost
dragged me under. I did everything
I could but refused the third demand.

Afterwards I paced the shores, the lanes,
the rooms, the streets,
cursing mothers and gods,
holding my drowned love in my arms again,

rescuing him in dream after dream
after dream.

That was the death that almost
took me down; before the event
I had unmasked symbiosis and I understood
the despairing music sucking me
downwards, downwards, over the edge,
madness demanding complement
even to the grave;
"You have one, but not two," I said
and clung to the Tree.

That was the death that slowed me;
I still dance but, if you know me well,
you sense the different quality,
the haunted pre-occupied air that strikes
without warning as though I was hearing
his death again, and resisting.

I am come here past seven deaths
to the promise of this sunny afternoon,
wind and bees in the basswoods,
blood summoned like sap
to the temples and the wrists

Tell me, my love, what deaths of yours
will deepen and darken these kisses?

Joan Finnigan

Stopping on Ice

Suddenly
        he was down—
his eyes strange, someone said,
mouth open—
      42 years old
coming back once a year
to the boys' game
        for charity,
a red-faced man with children
and a job and a mortgage.

      In 1949
he spent a playoff in the NHL
and that was as far as he got
in hockey
      but he died on the ice, seen
by 2000 people
      each one
catching a different angle
      a different moment,
their eyes drawn away from the puck
converging like rays of light
on the broken moment
      of his falling
2000 images
      laid
one on top the other so that
I see him falling
      over and over
going down in slow
      motion
his face
      like the boy's face
in tomorrow's newspaper, an Old Timer
playing for charity
      passing the goal
reaching for the post

```
                    missing
                            coasting
on out near the blue line
                        sinking
to his knees
            and reaching out
and falling—
                4000 eyes
seeing a boy who had his kidney
pierced by a skate at sixteen—
                            the red face
of the man darkening, sinking, gone now
as he fell to the silver ice
                        slowly
2000 times
            like a boy
falling
        and dying.
```

David Helwig

For John, Falling

Men stopped in the heel of sun,
hum of engines evaporated;
the machine displayed itself bellied with mud
and balanced—immense.

No one ran to where
his tensed muscles curled unusually,
where jaws collected blood,
the hole in his chest the size of fists,
hands clutched to eyes like a blindness.

Arched there he made
ridiculous requests for air.
And twelve construction workers
what should they do but surround
or examine the path of falling.

And the press in bright shirts,
a doctor, the foreman scuffing a mound,
men removing helmets,
the machine above him
shielding out the sun
while he drowned
in the beautiful dark orgasm of his mouth.

Michael Ondaatje

Far From the Shore

Is he dead? Is my friend dead?
Crasht, face against painted steel,
splattered with blood & needles of glass,
broken head splotcht with oily blood,
crusht bug of pavement-grinding crash,
lost coat & necktie twisted in mud?

Where is he now? That I hear his voice
        in my ear, urging he is alive, gentle face
    needing shave somewhere on land, white teeth
smiling at a world of air. Those teeth
        broken into half-rotted jags, strewn
    by uncaring night time hand, somewhere.

In a sky-blue casket, cast into the ground—
someone saw it, saw them do it, told me:
        I cant deny that, I cant deny last summer
    when I bought him a bottle of whiskey,
waved him away in Vancouver night,
the last time I saw him, away in a car,
        later off, to Ontario, what bleary clime.

& one month ago, filtered word, unwilling
    news, he is killed in auto wreck on far
        foreign highway—what sudden loom
in front of night, blazing lights in eyes,
desperate jag of heavy car, then, now,
        horrid air-filling explosion, shrieking steel,
            awkward shrapnel gouging into ground, a
twirling upside down rubber wheel, sirens.

All in the silence of my night here
    two thousand highway miles West, he was
often drunk, lay on floor at parties, eyes glazed
in utter joy & defiant empty bottle a scepter
    in his drunken white kingly hand, amused
        to the edge of his mouth, teeth in a second
    a light on his unshaven face, my friend,
        now mouldering—agh!—in the ground—

Handled by family & deacon, churchmen,
professionals, gravediggers, West Coast moist soil,
his body passt four miles from me

along westering railway, unknown, dead, baggage,
        making twenty minute stop in the night,
here, thru Calgary, on way to West Coast rot,
        & he wont get up!   this is country
of silent wind piling drift snow in
        Rocky Mountains, trenches of quiet death,
    lonely desolation, long wind-silent drift,
    thru deep black space, fall, langorous drug,

        fading, falling sleep thru night of space,
smiling teeth, faint among stars, gone, night,
        gone, further, Ian, my friend, where are you?

George Bowering

The Joy of Bones

Gently now the rain soaks the dead
In the quiet graveyard where they lie
It penetrates and washes them
Down to their white and shattered bones
And it frames out of their new clay
A sparse fragmented architecture
Strewn deep in dingy pits.

The dead are fine among the dead
For the dead rule in their own land
And there's but one joy there, the truth
Of their bones laid in eternity.

Georges Cartier

Translated from the French by Fred Cogswell

I Wanted to Write

I wanted to write a poem to death
But when it appeared envious
Like an old man seated in the sun
To warm up his already white bones
When it came amid waves of concrete
Flowers of steel drunken mobs
Long hair

I caught myself dancing before the mirror

Jacques Godbout

Translated from the French by H. Porter Abbott

The Dead

After we knew that we were dead we sat down and cried
   a little, only we found that our eyes were now empty
   and we were without any feeling of sadness.
"We had it coming, it was bound to happen," said one.
"I am thinking of the future," said a lady beside him.
"There is no future," an old man affirmed.
"I'm glad," said one, looking back toward the earth. "I'm
   free of it, I'm no longer one of them. I am glad."
"So am I," someone echoed.
"So am I."
"So am I . . . So am I," the echo traveled along the plain and
   beyond. I did not know whether it was an echo, or
   whether others were there repeating the sound.

175

"So am I, so am I" . . . it went on, the whole valley and plain resounded.

I turned my eyes around to see, but there was only a gray transparency without end, and empty, that was like a wall before me. I could see as far as I wanted but I wanted to see nothing, and there was nothing.

One of the dead beside me stirred, and as if a memory had awakened him he said, "They are always on edge down there. We were always on edge."

"And there was also the fear of death," said a man of middle age.

"Someone there dies every day, every hour.

Think of the bird in the teeth of the hunter, beating its wings, crying out—

That was the way we were." He fell into a deep silence. We all sat for a long time in silence.

Below us stretched the endless plain, and in the foreground, still near, the earth hung, like a sad town in a gray mist.

"There they sit, the beautiful women and the young men in their prime; time passes over them, and they shrivel in ugliness, looking at one another in amazement. O, I am glad to be out of it. Glad to be rid of it."

"But the worst is that even the innocent suffer," said a lady.

"They are all innocent," the old man muttered.

Then, raising his head, one poor skinflint beside me made a face like a devil who had done a good deed, and said, "All this is important. I never worried about important things. The worst of it was, as I see it now . . ." (he looked out across the plain into the gray distance without obstacle) "was to be caught in a net that did not even exist."

"When you are caught in a net," said the man of middle age, "whether it exists or doesn't exist, it is still a net, and you are caught in it."

"I don't even want to think of it," said the wizened man, as if losing interest;

"I remember," and here he bit his lip out of ancient habit, "that even love was painful."

And just as he said this, a dark cloud passed over us, and the earth was blotted out.

It brightened. But the figures beside me, and the earth that had formed a dark figure, receded, in no determinate direction, until I could see no longer. And then we were bathed in a morning light of sudden gladness. And there was nothing.

Louis Dudek

acknowledgements

The editor would like to thank H. Porter Abbott, Bruce Litteljohn, and Alan Whiteley for their advice and encouragement during the preparation of this book.

He is also grateful to the following publishers and authors for their kind permission to reproduce copyrighted material.

H. Porter Abbott: "The River" (after "Le fleuve" by Marcel Bélanger), "The Stranger in My Memory" (after "L'inconnue de ma mémoire" by Jean-Guy Pilon), "I'm Not Alone" (after "Je ne suis pas le seul et tout n'est pas fini" by Gilles Vigneault), and "I Wanted to Write" (after "Je voulais écrire" by Jacques Godbout), by permission.

Milton Acorn: "On Saint-Urbain Street" and "The Tolerant Philistine" from *I've Tasted My Blood*, by courtesy of the author.

Margaret Atwood: "Chronology" and "The Trappers" from *The Animals in That Country*, by permission of Oxford University Press, Canadian Branch; "The City Planners" and "Evening Trainstation Before Departure" from *The Circle Game*, © 1966, by permission of House of Anansi Press Limited.

Margaret Avison: "Banff," by permission.

Genevieve Bartole: "Breakup," by permission.

Henry Beissel: "Good Tidings and Goodwill in a Monsoon Drizzle" from *Face in the Dark*, © 1970 by the author, by permission of New Press; "The Blind Man," by permission; and "The Thrushes Do Not Die Out" (after "Die Drosseln sterben nicht aus" by Walter Bauer), by permission of the translator and Walter Bauer.

Earle Birney: "Daybreak on Lake Opal: High Rockies" from *What's So Big About Green;* "Bushed," "The Ebb Begins From Dream," "Oldster," and "Transcontinental" from *Selected Poems;* by permission of The Canadian Publishers, McClelland and Stewart Limited, Toronto.

bill bissett: "They Never Hurt No One But Yu Sure Have Mister and Missus Right in Canada" from *Nobody Owns th Earth*, © 1971, by permission of House of Anansi Press Limited.

George Bowering: "Grandfather" and "Far From the Shore" from *Touch*, by permission of The Canadian Publishers, McClelland and Stewart Limited, Toronto.

Michael Ondaatje: "Letters & Other Worlds" from *Rat Jelly* (The Coach House Press), © 1973, and "For John Falling" from *The Dainty Monsters* (The Coach House Press), © 1967. Copyright by the author, reprinted by permission.

P. K. Page: "Adolescence," "Foreigner," and "Masqueraders," by permission.

Al Purdy: "Idiot's Song" from *Love in a Burning Building;* "Homo Canadensis" from *The Cariboo Horses;* and "Home-Made Beer" from *Selected Poems;* by permission of The Canadian Publishers, McClelland and Stewart Limited, Toronto.

James Reaney: "The School Globe" from *Poems,* by permission of the author, Sybil Hutchinson, and New Press.

F. R. Scott: "Counter-Signs," "MacKenzie River," "Landscape Estranged" (after the poem by Roland Giguère), "The Closed Room" (after "La chambre fermée" by Anne Hébert), "Audacity," "The Examiner," "Knowing" (after "Connaissance" by Jacques Brault), "Poetry," and "The Clearing," by permission.

A. J. M. Smith: "The Lonely Land" and "On Knowing *Nothing*" from *Poems: New and Collected,* by permission of Oxford University Press, Canadian Branch.

Francis Sparshott: "A Protracted Affair" (after "Un amour au long cours" by Roland Giguère) from *A Cardboard Garage,* © 1969 by Clarke, Irwin & Company Limited, by permission.

Raymond Souster: "High Heels" from *Lost and Found,* © 1968 by Clarke, Irwin & Company Limited, by permission; "City Hall Street" from *The Colour of the Times* and "Jeanette" from *Ten Elephants on Yonge Street,* by permission of McGraw-Hill Ryerson Limited.

Tom Wayman: "Loneliness of the Unemployed," "The Ecology of Place," and "There's a Kind of Hush" from *Waiting for Wayman,* by permission of The Canadian Publishers, McClelland and Stewart Limited, Toronto.

Miriam Waddington: "Someone Who Used to Have Someone," by permission of the author; "Love Poem" from *Driving Home,* by permission of Oxford University Press, Canadian Branch.

George Woodcock: "Wider than Clouds" and "The Tramp" from *Selected Poems,* © 1967 by Clarke, Irwin & Company Limited, by permission.

J. Michael Yates: "Poem" from *Hunt in an Unmapped Interior,* by permission of the author and The Golden Quill Press.

Ian Young: "Any Man's History" and "Fear of the Landscape" from *Year of the Quiet Sun,* © 1969, by permission of the author and House of Anansi Press Limited.

Dale Zieroth: "Prairie Grade School," "Queen Street Trolley," and "Father" from *Clearing,* by permission.

Every effort has been made to make this list of acknowledgements complete, but in some cases all efforts to reach the copyright holder failed. All errors and omissions brought to the attention of the publisher will be corrected in future editions.

1 2 3 4 5 6   79 78 77 76 75   31149